"The only b   sitting.
It's a grippi   ust-share-
with-others book."
George Verwer, founder of Operation Mobilization

"*Total Abandon* is penetrating, honest, and touching. It captures a passion for following Jesus. Bonnie Witherall's martyrdom has touched many, but this book is about much more than her death. It's a powerful story of God calling His people to serve, suffer, trust, and find joy and purpose. May the story of Gary and Bonnie Witherall challenge, deepen, and rekindle the fire of first love."
Randy Alcorn, author of *Safely Home* and *Heaven*

"Gary has put into words the unspeakable horror Bonnie suffered and he endured. But the heart of this remarkable book is not horror, but hope. Rarely are the stories we most badly need to hear told so well."
Michael Card, musician, author, and songwriter

"It is not what they do for God but what he does for them that distinguish Christ's true followers. He gives peace when terror would be the natural response, love when he allows the enemy to take the life of one of his sheep. Gary tells what happened when terrorists killed his wife; God is writing the rest of the story."
Steve Saint, author of *End of the Spear*

"Reaching the Lebanese for Christ cost Bonnie her life, which was not lived in vain. May her story cause us to follow in her steps to be 'faithful until death,' knowing we will one day join the ranks before God's throne partaking in the 'crown of life' (Revelation 2:10)."
Tom White, U.S. director, The Voice of the Martyrs

"As a young boy growing up in Argentina, my mother used to stress to me the importance of reading stories of dynamic missionary work. *Total Abandon* is such a story. It is a must-read for every believer who longs for meaningful, active faith in Christ. Gary and Bonnie Witherall were completely committed to Christ, even when it cost them everything. Every person who has heard God's call on their life—whether for overseas missions or service here at home—needs to read this story."

Luis Palau, Luis Palau Evangelistic Association

TOTAL ABANDON

GARY WITHERALL
with Elizabeth Cody Newenhuyse

TYNDALE HOUSE PUBLISHERS, INC.
WHEATON, ILLINOIS

Visit Tyndale's exciting Web site at www.tyndale.com

TYNDALE is a registered trademark of Tyndale House Publishers, Inc. Tyndale's quill logo is a trademark of Tyndale House Publishers, Inc.

Total Abandon

Library of Congress Cataloging-in-Publication Data

Witherall, Gary.
  Total abandon / Gary Witherall with Elizabeth Cody Newenhuyse.
    p. cm.
  ISBN-13: 978-0-8423-8899-3
  ISBN-10: 0-8423-8899-0
  1. Witherall, Bonnie Penner, d. 2002. 2. Witherall, Gary. 3. Missionaries—
Lebanon—Biography. 4. Missions—Lebanon. I. Newenhuyse, Elizabeth Cody. II. Title.
  BV3210.L4W58 2005
  266'.0092—dc22   2005013945

Printed in the United States of America

10 09 08 07 06 05
 7   6   5   4   3   2   1

For Bonnie

Contents

FOREWORD

Dr. Joseph Stowell

I've heard gripping stories of martyrs all of my life. In fact, *Foxe's Book of Martyrs* was an early assignment on our family reading list. The story of John and Betty Stam, who gave their lives for Christ in China, has often made it into messages that I have preached about courage and commitment. The murder of the five missionaries in the jungles of Ecuador made an indelible mark on my life as a young boy. More recently, reports from Vietnam, Sudan, and hostile Muslim countries have reminded us that martyrdom is not just a thing of the past. In fact, it is now being reported that more followers of Christ have been murdered for their faith in the last century than in all of church history combined.

But in spite of my interest in the unique courage of Christians who gave their lives for Christ, I never thought that I would know a martyr personally. Or, I should say, have the honor of having known this kind of courageous Christian.

It was a day like any other in my work at Moody Bible Institute when my assistant interrupted a rather routine administrative meeting with the shocking news that Bonnie Witherall had been shot and killed in Sidon, Lebanon. The details were sketchy, but in those initial reports there was already the sense that this was not just a random street shooting.

Given the size of our student body, I don't have the opportunity to know all of our students well. Gary and Bonnie were exceptions.

A flood of memories filled my head, and a deep sadness weighed heavily on my spirit. I had known both Bonnie and her husband, Gary, as students at MBI.

Gary was a hip and energetic international student from the United Kingdom. Bonnie was striking in her love for people and warm personality. Neither of them were average. Gary was a stand-out on the soccer team and carried a zeal and passion for evangelism that stemmed from his precollege experience with Operation Mobilization.

I knew Bonnie best as a nanny who often baby-sat for a couple who lived a few floors above us in the Chicago high-rise my wife, Martie, and I were in at the time. Connecting with the busy city people who lived above and below us was often nothing more than sharing a ride on the elevator. But Bonnie's life had been a bridge that opened many opportunities for us. Her radiance and integrity made a deep impression on the people in our building. They would often say to me how much they loved Bonnie and that if all our students were like her, then Moody must be a very special place. It was her love and devotion to Christ that showed up consistently with everyone she came into contact with. She had, on occasion, baby-sat for our grandchildren as well. So you can imagine the impact that the shocking news about Bonnie made on my heart.

As the reports became more complete, it became increasingly clear that Bonnie had died for the cause of the gospel. She was living proof that Jesus was not only worth living for, but worth dying for as well.

In the days that followed, nearly every national newspaper and media outlet was on our campus interviewing our students about how they felt about serving Christ now that a fellow student had been brutally murdered in a foreign land. The testimony rang loud and clear that Bonnie's death had only strengthened their resolve to carry the gospel wherever they were led. A major article in the *New York Times* highlighted the life and testimony of Bonnie and our students' response to the tragedy. In those early days, it was becoming clear that Bonnie's death was already multiplying the gospel far beyond the influence of her quiet, yet important ministry in Lebanon.

Her crime? Showing the love of Christ to refugees and children in a medical facility and shelter in what both she and Gary knew was a dangerous country. Her honor? To give her life for the Savior who had given his life for her.

I don't know why Christ requires some of our brightest and best—sometimes in the vibrancy of their youth. But He often does. And while I will trust Him that He knows best, I will also be grateful that for a brief time in my life I had the privilege of knowing personally one whom God counted worthy to be numbered among the martyrs.

Gary tells the story best. You will hang on every word. But my prayer is that this will be far more than a gripping story for you. It is my prayer that because you have read this book, you will be far more willing to live courageously and with a fresh commitment to the high calling of being a follower of Christ . . . regardless.

✝

Come out for God and say: "Lord, anything for Thee." If you say that with prayer, and speak that into God's ear, He will accept it, and He will teach you what it means.

—*Andrew Murray, Absolute Surrender*

I was reading Psalm 37 today and one verse in particular spoke to me; it's verse 32. "The wicked lie in wait for the righteous, seeking their very lives; but the Lord will not leave them in their power or let them be condemned when [they are] brought to trial."

—*From Bonnie's journal: November 16, 2002*

1

A WORLD ENDS

*God, You are the Lord of our circumstances. We did not
come to Lebanon by accident—we are exactly where You
meant for us to be. Lord, I want to worship You in the
place where You've put me today. Help me to remember
these four words: "This is My doing."*
— From Bonnie's journal: February 2002

Sidon, Lebanon: November 21, 2002

I thought it was someone laughing on the answering machine.

Bonnie had left early as usual for the clinic where she worked
assisting poor, pregnant Palestinian women. It was my day off and,
night person that I am, I was contentedly sleeping in, happy for a
respite from the busyness of our lives ministering in the southern
Lebanon city of Sidon. The phone rang about 8 a.m. in our apartment overlooking the Mediterranean Sea. After two rings, the
answering machine came on. I heard a shrieking, garbled voice on
the line—it sounded almost like hideous laughter. At first I thought
it was someone joking around, but then I recognized the voice of

Bonnie's coworker Alison, pleading with me to get to the clinic. I jumped out of bed and rushed to hit the replay button. As I listened, my world ended. Her call was no joke; instead it filled me with horror and panic. I needed to get to the clinic, fast.

It's strange how trivial details stand out at a time when the planet seems to be spinning out of control. I dressed and looked for the one thousand Lebanese lire (equivalent to seventy cents American) for a taxi fare across town. Desperately I pawed through all the drawers, looking for money in the money-management envelope system we had adopted from a Larry Burkett book. I pulled out a couple of notes and raced down the seven flights of stairs out to the main road. What I did notice was that on this November day the sun was shining, the air warm.

Traffic streamed along our beachside road. I hailed a cab and asked the driver to take me to the other side of town, directing him toward a well-known candy store we regularly cited as a landmark for the drivers. In keeping with the city's air of shopworn elegance, the cab, like most of the taxis, was an older Mercedes-Benz, pocked with dents, leather interior worn. Yet I knew the driver was extremely proud of his car, considering it a beloved old friend. He navigated slowly, weaving through traffic and cutting other cars off. We drove through the main downtown square of Sidon, which at Ramadan and Christmas is festooned with lights.

As we neared the clinic, the driver decided to stop and fill up the cab's gas tank. It had already been a slow ride, and my anxiety was mounting. Slow was the normal pace in Lebanon; the driver had no idea what I was going through. As he pulled into the station, two other taxis were also waiting. I realized it would be a good wait to get to the pumps, so I paid the driver and began running. It was close to a half-mile sprint. People rarely run in the Middle East, so I stood out. My panic grew as I ran—although I fought off the fear, telling myself, *It can't be anything that bad. Can it?*

I finally made it to the road of the clinic where Bonnie had spent more than a year bringing love and mercy to Palestinian women who knew little of either. My adrenaline surged, propelling me down the dusty street. That moment on the bright Mediterranean morning, little more than a year after 9/11, days before Thanksgiving would be celebrated in America, was surreal: I was running through a city few have heard of or will ever see, running to my wife's side to protect her, running for my life, running for her life.

I thought of the children we planned to have and how we wanted to grow old happily together. I thought of the way Bonnie's face was changing and maturing—*Oh, how much I loved that face.*
Then my mind flashed back to Portland, Oregon, and all the peaceful evenings we had spent on our balcony with the cool summer breeze blowing through the tree branches as we sat quietly drinking coffee, laughing, and playing Scrabble. Oregon seemed very far away, a place we gave up to love the hurting and unloved in the world. If we had stayed, by this time we could have already built a beautiful house in the hills, among the trees. But we simply could not ignore the call to bring a message of hope and forgiveness to a world devastated by hate and war.

As I approached, I saw our car parked outside the church where the clinic was located, just as Bonnie had left it, and an ambulance without lights on. *Why was it here? Had Bonnie miscarried again?*
Fear was spiraling into terror. I reached the front gate and a young soldier raised his AK-47 at me, telling me I could not enter. He was slight of build and his face registered shock. Perhaps he had been brought up in some village in Lebanon, hearing a lifetime of stories about the civil war that had ravaged the country in the 1970s and

'80s. I pushed him aside, thinking he might just shoot me, but I would take that chance. I ran through the heavy black steel gate with fear pounding in my soul.

The clinic was located on the second floor of a small evangelical church. On the third floor was a home for foreign workers where you could always find a place for in-depth conversations over great food and strong, acidic Arabic coffee. The building had been there for many years, since well before the war when it was part of a thriving Christian community. But as was true of most areas in Lebanon, many of the believers here had fled or died in the war. Mosques surrounding the area seemed to defiantly point their loudspeakers right toward this little church. Their messages of political anguish saturated everything; it fell on the streets and into every house. The Palestinian *intifada* was in full swing, so there was always reason to broadcast more than the call to prayer. But inside the church, away from the clamor, it was peaceful. Here, where Jesus' words—I am the way and the truth and the life. No one comes to the Father except through me (John 14:6)—are carved in wood above three arched windows, Muslims were always welcome, to be friends and cross the barriers of hate and fear.

Lebanon could be described as a tolerance zone in a region fractured by hatred and violence. Although the civil war is over, peace remains tenuous between Christians and Muslims—for many Christians, Islam seems to be becoming more and more victorious.

I ran up the stairs, the same steps where women came for help, the same steps where the local Christians gathered, where many people from Sidon came to learn English. It was where children were able to find a warm, safe environment. At the top of the stairs, two large soldiers grabbed hold of me. I twisted around to see through the clinic door and caught a glimpse of Bonnie's legs on the floor inside the reception area. I tried to see more but they ripped my hands from the door frame and pushed me onto the floor in the next room. The soldiers were protecting me from the horror of what had happened.

One of the believers in the room who had arrived before I did tried to calm me down. He quickly handed me a white plastic cup of water. I pushed him away and the water splashed across the room. What was he thinking? that I was thirsty? that water would help me calm down?

"What's wrong?" I yelled to no one in particular. "What's happening? Let me see my wife!"

2

A SCHOOL, A CITY, A WOMAN

My mind, soul, and being have been thrown into new depths as I have come face-to-face with a girl that I knew nothing about. . . . This female is different from so many I have met. She exudes life—and inspires it in me. She motivates me. I feel very tense and on the edge, but also calm and peaceful. The amazing thing is that she is equally struck by me.

—From Gary's journal: May 7, 1996

Repeatedly people have asked me, "Weren't you afraid to go to the Middle East?" And my answer has been, "Well, you're at risk walking in downtown Chicago at night, too." I should know.

It was late December 1994. I had been at Moody Bible Institute three years and was walking one night to a friend's apartment on Oak Street, not far from the notorious Cabrini-Green housing projects, a dense cluster of high-rise buildings where violence, gang activity, and drug trafficking was the norm. Cabrini-Green was just a couple of blocks from the MBI campus. I always found it amazing that I could walk a few blocks east to the lake and find some of the most luxurious real estate in America—then go west and find the direst sort of poverty, hopelessness, and crime. To their credit, Moody students are involved in many ministries with Cabrini residents: tutoring programs, big-sister and big-brother activities, and sports.

On this night, close to Christmas, it was freezing cold; in the air hung what I can only call a city smell—you know it if you've smelled it. It's the combination of car exhaust, cold, American and ethnic food cooking, smoke from a million furnaces, and, in Chicago, the water of Lake Michigan. I walked along feeling streetwise and confident. Suddenly I noticed two guys behind me in athletic apparel. One asked me what time it was. As I turned to look at my watch, I saw a big shiny pistol pointing at me. He started screaming and cursing and then thrust the gun into my kidneys. He wanted everything. His partner took my watch, my wallet, my bag. He even wanted my jacket and my shoes. When I turned toward him, he cursed at me and told me to look away. "Hey, I'm from Moody," I said. "I come here all the time. We're involved in helping the kids."

I was shocked at what happened next. The robber stopped for a moment and stood back, his long arms—and the gun—raised to the sky. He started cursing and said, "I was going to mess you up! You're lucky you told me that. I'm sorry, man."

After they gave everything back to me, the two men turned and started walking toward the projects. The gunman waved his gun in the air and said, "Forget this ever happened. Sorry, man."

The whole time during the robbery I was preparing to be shot or even killed. Yet somehow in the moment I had peace and freely offered everything. I even asked the robber if he would like me to help him in some way.

Soon after he left I started to shake. A police car came by, stopped, and the officer jumped out. I told him what had just taken place. "I've been on the force for years and have never heard of anything like this," he said. He was surprised that the robber chose not to rob me, as if he had distinguished me from those he despised.

I didn't tell many people about the incident. Deep within I believed the Lord had protected me from harm, somehow softening the heart of this thug who carried a big handgun. I also realized that this was an example of how years of loving the unloved—as Moody does—has an impact. Moody has had opportunities to move to the suburbs, but the institution is committed to making a difference in the urban environment. And despite the increasing affluence and new construction in the neighborhood in recent years, the human need is always there: the homeless, elderly people garbage-picking, prostitutes, drug addicts. And prisoners.

While at Moody I had the opportunity to work in Cook County Jail in Section 6, the maximum-security area for men awaiting trial or sentenced to the state penitentiary. These inmates faced lives of bleakness, danger, and hopelessness. Prison life is brutal, chaotic, and dehumanizing. Yet many find the gospel in a powerful way—or the gospel finds them. Simply put, Jesus gives hope to the hopeless.

I joined a Bible study group of about thirty men. Most were African American; all wore khaki shirts and pants. I can still remember the smell of incarceration. I had smelled it before—in Hong Kong, where I visited a maximum-security prison on a desolate island. The Cook County Jail is right in the city, on the west side of Chicago's Loop, but it, too, is a desolate island.

One night I was asked if I would meet with Lawrence, one of the Latino inmates. When I first met him he was strung out on drugs. I remember asking him if he knew why there was a rainbow in the sky. "No," he replied. In fact, he knew almost nothing about the Bible, even though he called himself a Christian. So I offered to take him through the Bible just as I had learned to do myself at Moody. We met once a week for several months. When I came back the following year he was so excited to see me. He told me that he had given his life to Christ and was now memorizing Scripture. But what meant the most was that he called me "brother."

Spring 1996: There came a time in my life where I just did not want to be alone anymore. I wanted to share my life with someone. I wanted to share the Good News about Jesus around the world and I needed a special person to do it alongside me. The right person. After struggling and failing at dating, I asked the Lord to bring someone into my life. And in the meantime I wrote her, that future someone, a letter:

> *February 14, 1996*
>
> *To my beloved,*
> *Hey, what's up? It is a science class I'm sitting in, listening to a study on carbon.*
> *I wonder where you are and what you are doing, or even if you exist. I pray for you all the time. However, I*

feel like no one is able to touch my emotions and the
person behind the walls of my personal life. But as I
have discovered once before, I am not a rock and my
heart can be hurt.

Well, happy Valentine's Day. Hey, wherever you are,
come and find me. I will be thirty in April and I gradu-
ate in May. I think I am going to return to Operation
Mobilization, although I am not sure yet. But I am
excited about what God has in store. I wonder if we
know each other.

> *Lord protect you today,*
> *Gary*

Over spring break I flew down to the Operation Mobilization offices in Atlanta. Operation Mobilization is a Christian organization that is committed to bringing the love of Jesus to the world. Over four thousand workers serve with OM around the world, including its two ships—the MV *Doulos* and MV *Logos II*. I had already worked nearly four years on the ships before coming to Moody, and recently I had met with some leaders expressing my desire to return to the ships when I finished my schooling. A few weeks later I received a letter from the leadership of the ships ministry, inviting me to head up the evangelism department on the MV *Doulos*. I would fly out to Japan to meet the ship in October.

I was so excited! I could not have hoped for better news. I ran up to my dorm floor and showed the letter to the other guys. God was in control, and suddenly I had direction. I now knew He was leading me back to Operation Mobilization to focus on evangelism. And for the moment, as a single man.

April 26, 1996

Dear Wife,

Will I ever meet you? I don't know. But hello. This year is full of emotion for me. Mostly good, but here I stand on the threshold of a great new experience with OM mission. I am excited to see what will happen. I just turned thirty and actually feel good about it.

Dancing in the Rain

The first time I met her was in the plaza at Moody Bible Institute. I was walking from class one day, and she smiled at me. I smiled back and said, "I'm sorry, I don't know your name!" Her hazel eyes flashed as she retorted, "That's because you never asked me!"

She later told me she had been secretly interested in getting to know me for a long time; we were in many of the same classes. But I had been totally unaware. I had failed in past relationships and now I was afraid. Because I only wanted to give my heart to the one I would marry, I did not want to complicate my life with just another woman.

Our world religions class went on a field trip to visit a Hindu temple. I had spent six months in India and was familiar with Hinduism. I had seen firsthand how it keeps millions of people poor and oppressed. There in the temple with my Moody classmates, standing next to Krishna as I listened to a boring old priest drone on, I brooded about all the religions, all the gods, all the killing and persecution, the suffering of the church even today in India. The martyrs.

And there was Bonnie, smiling at me, saying, "Does this make you want to sing 'My Sweet Lord' by George Harrison?" I said no , this place upsets me. We began to tell each other how God had directed our lives. She told me she was interested in Youth With a Mission's (YWAM) ship ministry! This woman knew how to get my attention.

A week later we bumped into each other in the student dining hall. We sat, stared at each other, and told each other our stories. I felt like I was talking to a princess. I told Bonnie, "Whoever I marry, I want to help her succeed to be her very best. I don't want her to just follow me."

It seemed we had found each other. In this world of loneliness, of endlessly trying to figure things out, she was there in front of me, and I was not going to let her go.

Because of this, I wanted to protect the relationship and not ruin it by playing a thoughtless dating game. So I told her, "Any time you call me, we can go out, but I'm not going to call you." She agreed. We spent the next two weeks together, and sparks flew.

Chicago is an amazing place to fall in love—a city of restaurants, coffee shops, parks, and pan pizza. We spent a lot of time in a little coffee shop called The Wolf and Kettle on the campus of Loyola University. Bonnie and I both loved books and coffee shops. She especially loved Russian literature, and our conversations would range from the current books we were reading to adventurous explorations of how we could impact the world.

One day we were caught in a heavy downpour in the city. Instead of following me to take cover under a store awning, Bonnie ran into the middle of the street and danced in the rain. She was wearing a black dress, and she was celebrating. Life was good, and we knew this was it for us.

Over the summer I went to Michigan to work in a youth camp, as I had done a couple of years before. After a few weeks, Bonnie came up to help in one of the camps for special-needs people. It seemed that everywhere she went in the camp, Bonnie always had a couple of girls hanging around her. She naturally warmed to them, and they to her. While we were at camp, she wrote her first love letter to me.

Dearest love,

I'm sitting here after having just been with you—missing you. Not the bad missing you, but the good missing you. My love . . . I love you. I have made a choice; I don't think you could do anything to make that change. I want to be a secure, peaceful, calm strength for you. I desire to stand by you whatever you do, to be your soul mate, your friend, and your lover. I want to be your woman and you to be my man. I am proud of you. I trust you and depend on you. Gary, I need your love and am totally confident in you. You're my hero. Please don't doubt my love for you. I accept you 100 percent. There is nothing about you that I don't accept and cherish. My darling, I pray that the Lord gives many days for us to learn and express our love to one another.

I want to give you a passage that really encouraged me today. It's Ecclesiastes 4:9-12:

"Two are better than one, because they have a good return for their work: If one falls down, his friend can help him up. But pity the man who falls and has no one to help him up! Also, if two lie down together, they will keep warm. But how can one keep warm alone? Though one may be overpowered, two can defend themselves. A cord of three strands is not quickly broken."

Gary, please know that when I'm with my ladies today that I am also thinking of you. When I look across the crowd I feel love for you and long to hold you and touch you. And kiss you.

My heart longs to be with you always.

Love,

Bonnie

(your little lady)

I tucked the note in my wallet—where it remained throughout our marriage.

What Now?

Now decisions loomed. Summer was winding down. I was headed for the *Doulos*—but here this curly-haired princess had shown up. I was torn. Bonnie was graduating that December; perhaps she could fly out and meet me in January. But I had a three-year commitment. Should we date that whole time? It would be, at best, a distraction for me and unfair to her.

I called Richard Sharp, a mentor who had known me since my days on the ships, and explained the dilemma. "I don't think it's a good idea to wait that long," he said. "Why don't you hold off on the ships for a while and get married?"

I saw the wisdom of his counsel. I needed to put Bonnie first, before my own career. This was a formative choice, one that laid the foundation for our entire relationship. In the years to come, we always considered how something might affect the other person before making decisions.

So rather than sailing the world again, I spent the fall of 1996 walking Michigan Avenue, working at Eddie Bauer, the upscale clothing and outdoor-gear merchant, and also Rand McNally, where maps, globes, and other travel-related items are sold. I lived with friends near the airport and in the evenings would meet up with Bonnie. We gravitated to coffee shops where she did her homework and I tried to distract her.

December in Chicago usually brings snow and freezing winds. This year was no different. Six days before Christmas I went to a car-rental place. I had called ahead and paid for an economy-sized car, but when I told the woman at the counter what it was for she upgraded me to a larger, cherry-red Oldsmobile 88. I picked Bonnie up and drove her to Navy Pier, the Chicago skyline twinkling behind us like a stage set. I had bought a beautiful ring, which I had nervously been fingering in my pocket all day. We sat for a moment on a bench, our faces turning red from the wintry wind off the lake. "I'm cold," Bonnie said. "Let's go back to the car."

I quickly knelt down, presented her with the ring, and asked her to marry me. She jumped up and said, "Yes!" laughing loudly.

"I'm getting married!" she cried to the world.

As we hugged, a photographer on the Pier saw us as he was capturing the city at night.

We both had just completed four years of Bible schooling. There had been some wonderful years and some tough experiences, learning about life and purpose. The Lord had brought us together and now we couldn't contain our excitement over where God would lead us. Bonnie and I were two people who loved Jesus and longed to live for Him completely. Even though we both had struggles in life, we shared the same passion to share His love with a hurting world.

Our stories each began in places with green landscapes, thousands of miles apart. I'll begin with mine. . . .

3

THERE MUST BE MORE

I cannot shake a Bible verse that I have been thinking over . . .
"Our gospel came to you not simply with words, but also
with power, with the Holy Spirit and with deep conviction"
(1 Thessalonians 1:5, NIV*). Christian institutions are so good*
at the "word" aspect and yet sometime can neglect the rest.
To bring Jesus into the picture brings the fire. LORD, LIGHT
ME UP! —*From Gary's journal: March 2003*

Once there was a quiet, kind, and green world, a world where I felt
wholly safe. Yet seared in the older generation's mind were memories of exploding bombs blitzing the seacoast contrasted with a
world where, in spring, the moors were carpeted with bluebells
and in summer, the twilights were long. It was a world where on
winter nights I lay listening to the gales off the English Channel
rattling the four-paned windows in our old house while next to
me my cat purred.

This was the world I would eventually leave to go adventuring for Christ. Unbeknownst to me at the time, of course, Bonnie Penner was growing up halfway across the world in an equally green and tranquil corner of the United States, on a hill in a place called Washington—but we're getting ahead of the story.

My family lived in a coal-heated gray Victorian terrace (row) house located on a quiet road. I remember being fascinated by the rag-and-bone man who occasionally roamed the area with his horse and carriage, looking for anything he might sell. Great social forces were buffeting the old order in the world beyond; but my world growing up in Devon, near the sea, was circumscribed by narrow lanes, windy moors, and towering oak trees—the trees whose timbers built the great ships in the Royal Navy's golden age when England ruled the waves. Even today, Devon is dotted with old churches, picturesque farmsteads, grazing cattle, and flocks of sheep. It isn't unusual to see a shepherd and his dogs stopping traffic as they drive the flock over the hills of Dartmoor (now a national park). High hedgerows dividing the fields defined ancient feudal plots.

Equally ancient was the parish church I sang in as a choirboy. St. Mary's, built in medieval times, had been an Augustinian priory before Henry VIII dissolved the monasteries in the sixteenth century. My parents were married there; and now my grandparents are buried there in the same churchyard my granddad tended as gardener after his retirement from his career as a train engineer. I loved the stained-glass windows in St. Mary's—especially the way the deep blues and reds would diffract the light on sunny Sundays. The large stone pillars rose grandly into arches supporting the intricately carved roof of dark wood; flags from past wars and ornate banners decorated the walls. The organist grandly commanded joyful sounds out of the hymns as we sang our hearts out. On Saturdays I would get paid twenty-five pence to sing at weddings.

I met Jesus—or, more accurately, He met me—when I was six. My parents, who had recently become Christians, sent me to a children's youth camp. At six years old, I felt I was a pretty good kid, but the invitation the preacher gave to the campers, to confess the sin in our hearts and journey through life with Jesus, compelled me—and set me on the first steps toward an adventure with Him.

Living near the sea, adventure always beckoned on the wind. My dad had served in the Royal Navy, and I loved his stories of seafaring. I always imagined I would follow in his footsteps someday. One hot summer day I remember swimming in the sea with my family, watching the ships leave from the harbor nearby. One vessel passed us, reflecting the sun as it moved slowly out of the harbor toward the channel. I could make out the sailors standing at the bow, leaning over the side. I wondered what they were talking about as they watched the skyline of Plymouth slowly fade into the haze. *Where was she going?* I wondered. *What would it be like to disappear over that horizon and see what was on the other side?*

When I was ten, we moved east to a town called Crawley, in Sussex, just southwest of London. Crawley grew from a consolidation of neighboring villages to a town after the destruction of London in World War II. I loved visiting with my grandparents over a lovely cup of English tea. Sometimes they told amazing stories about planes in dogfights and hearing the V-1s, the unmanned flying bombs, scream overhead. The German rockets were aimed at London but would sometimes run out of fuel before hitting the target and land in nearby fields.

Another, much older historical landmark was located just a mile or so from our house. Worth Church was built in AD 890, before the Norman Conquest. My sister was recently married there. The ancient church is an image of the old England I knew: a symbol of the way things were until recent times.

Another Brick in the Wall

Far from the moors, far from the peaceful world of my childhood, the anarchy and anger of the punk rock movement swept the United Kingdom in the late 1970s and '80s. Like my peers, I became caught up in the music, so much so that it began to change the way I viewed life. Pink Floyd's cynical anthem, "Another Brick in the Wall," became a soundtrack for the era. Without realizing what was happening, I was being swept toward a dismal future.

I began to distance myself from my family and wonder about my future: Was my destiny to be "another brick in the wall," making machine parts on some meaningless factory floor? School was a bore. Mr. Wray, the headmaster, would pray in our morning assembly (a requirement of the state church system), but to the students he showed little to no faith in God. For him, it was perhaps an exercise in being British. It seemed, as well, that he was always caning students, whacking them with his ruler if they stepped out of line. I made it my goal not to be one of them. Slowly I began hating school life.

My required religion classes weren't any better: Our professor, Mr. Bishop, would constantly lose his temper and slam the books on his desk in a fit of rage. He was a very unhappy man. The kids ended up mocking him, and he would retaliate by throwing chalk or the eraser at the class. His behavior epitomized the line in "Another Brick in the Wall": *Teacher, leave those kids alone. . . .* To me he demonstrated neither kindness nor respect.

It was in this kind of environment that my friends were being exposed to the person and message of Jesus. Is it any wonder that it took only a few generations for the English population, en masse, to reject Christianity?

Although I went to church, I found it hard to reconcile Jesus, Christianity, and the culture I was getting wrapped up in. I wanted to do something great in life but saw little to look forward to in the future.

One day as I was sitting in history class, completely bored, I looked out the window, thinking, *Is there something out there for me?* I felt alone. Nothing in my life seemed to matter. Not only was I drifting away from my family, I was drifting away from Jesus.

There was one thing I still enjoyed, though. I had been an avid bicyclist for years, going on long rides every weekend. But when I turned sixteen, I walked into a motorbike store and drove away on a 50cc off-road moped—a yellow Suzuki. I loved that bike! Suddenly I was mobile; suddenly I was able to go out in the evenings and meet up with friends. Bikes were the craze; bikes were cool; bikes were a way out of our meaningless lives. We would do everything possible to make them go faster. Eventually I upgraded to a bigger bike, 100cc. It was able to go over 60 mph. Although it was dangerous, my friends and I would race on the streets late at night.

Risking my life was thrilling—and the truth was, I really didn't care anymore. One October afternoon, when I was seventeen, I was tearing down the hill on my bike in front of our school. I was going as fast as possible, showing off for the crowds of kids getting out of school, enjoying the exhilaration. I whisked under a railway bridge, turned a sharp bend at full speed, only to see an oncoming car squeezing between the cars parked on both sides of the road.

I had nowhere to go. In a flash I decided my only option was to brake hard and slam into the back of one of the parked cars. Just before impact, my whole life flashed before me, not only my past, but the future that would never be. I saw the girl I would never marry, the family I would never have. I hit the curb, flew off the bike, hit the back of the parked car, and went airborne, past a street lamp, just missing a tree, and finally landing on a grassy strip thirty feet away. Both the bike and the car were totaled. I lay on my back; my leg, badly broken and twisted, throbbed in agonizing pain. In my panic I couldn't tell what injuries I actually had sustained. Then the pain surged through my arm as I became aware that my hand hurt—my thumb had been completely bent backward and the bone snapped as my hand was forced from the accelerator lever.

I think I probably blacked out when I was catapulted from the bike and then regained consciousness on landing. The first person I saw when I looked up was my old home economics teacher, a large Dutch lady with a pronounced accent. She had blessed my life by teaching me how to make cookies. I looked at her in a dreamlike half-stupor as the screaming pain in my twisted leg began to demand my full attention.

One of my close friends was walking home from school at the time and had watched the whole thing in horror. Steve just remembers the *thump* of the impact. He and a group of other friends came racing over. Gasoline from the bike's gas tank was spilling on the road. Steve found the gas cap, closed the tank, ran over and said, "It's okay, Gary. I turned the petrol off." This has been our joke for years.

It seemed like forever before the ambulance arrived. I thought I was going to die and began to hyperventilate. The paramedics had to cut my new cord jeans in order to put me in traction. Even then, through the fog of pain, nearing the end of my life (so I thought), I felt a quick stab of disappointment—*I just bought these jeans!* Steve jumped in the back of the ambulance with me, and sirens blaring, we sped to Cuckfield hospital. I passed out on the way, but do remember telling the rescue team, "I'm going to heaven because I believe in Jesus."

The next thing I remember is seeing my parents as I was about to go into surgery. Weeping, I said, "I'm sorry." I later learned just how seriously I was hurt: I had needed six pints of blood and seven pints of plasma to replenish what I had lost.

A couple of days later I regained consciousness. I awoke naked, covered only by a thin blanket, on a gurney being wheeled from intensive care into a ward full of other boys who had also been injured in accidents. My leg was still in traction—suspended in air by bits of metal.

Before long we began to swap stories in the ward. One of the patients, an old school friend, had several screws in his leg because it had shattered into small pieces. Another guy was in a bed that was regularly rotated. Even his head was secured.

One day a lady who was visiting someone accidentally knocked the pulley weight stabilizing my leg with her purse, jarring the traction apparatus and my leg. The pain was so excruciating, I can still remember it vividly.

A few days later I went back into surgery in order to rebuild my leg by putting a long rod through the center of the bone. Two screws held a piece of bone that had broken off. This surgery took over six hours. Within days I was given some crutches. I refused to use a wheelchair; nothing terrified me more than the possibility of not walking again. I became intensely focused on making a full recovery.

One day I opened a Bible my dad had left next to me. The pages flipped open to the Magnificat—the passage in Luke's Gospel where Mary praises God for His wonderful work in using her as His servant to bear His Son. I began to cry, overwhelmed with gratitude to God for the fact that He allowed me to live. There on that hospital cot I told the Lord, "As You have given life back to me, I now dedicate my life to You."

With that prayer, everything changed.

War and Peace

I decided to let go of everything to follow the Lord. It was exciting to draw closer to Him; still, I made a lot of mistakes. Aden, my youth leader at the time, would see me coming and say, "What is it this time?" He fondly dubbed me "Witherbrain" because I tended to proceed without thinking and often ended up making bad decisions. Even though I was immature and had a lot to learn, Aden saw something in my life and decided to invest himself in me. Through the years, he has closely followed the results of that investment.

I had always wanted to serve in the military. A couple of my uncles were in the marines and had served in Northern Ireland while my father had traveled the world in the Royal Navy. I thought that joining the military would be a great way to journey beyond the borders of the world I knew.

Only weeks after my bike accident, a Christian ministry ship docked in Brighton on the south coast. My youth group took a bus to Brighton so we could tour the ship and learn about the ministry. I never anticipated how this day would change my life. It was late in the year, and the weather was overcast, but I couldn't pass up this opportunity. When I boarded the *MV Logos*, it was like I had entered a whole new world. The ship was staffed by Christians who traveled around the world sharing the good news of Jesus. They had a big book exhibition and conference room where several gave their testimonies. It seemed too good to be true! I had become jaded about Christians, thinking that they never seemed to do any-thing very well. Yet here was an amazing ship, dedicated to help-ing—not harming—others.

The previous year, 1982, Britain was at war with Argentina, fighting over some windswept little islands off the South American coast—the Falklands—that were home to more sheep than people. The British had claimed the Falklands in 1833 (after earlier wars with Spain and Argentina) and established a colonial administra-tion in 1842. Yet Argentina maintained that the islands belonged to them, and so they invaded with a large force. The British, under Prime Minister Margaret Thatcher's leadership, responded quickly with superior air and naval forces.

One of my friends was on a military ship called the HMS *Glamorgan*. The Argentine planes launched a heat-seeking missile that slammed through the helicopter hangar onboard the *Glamorgan* and straight into the galleys, killing several men. My friend Andy, who had lived across the street from us in Sussex, was about to take his shift in the galley when the tragedy happened. Returning to the U.K. he became disillusioned; for him, war was not pretty. I was shocked to learn about a British sub that sank an Argentinean ship called the *Belgrano*. This ship had been full of young men forced into the military. Hundreds died. *Why?* I won-dered. As I considered the realities of war, I realized that joining the navy no longer had the same appeal. Instead, the work of the OM ships began to look more interesting.

Called Out

About that same time, Melody Green, the widow of American Christian singer/songwriter Keith Green, was ministering in the U.K. She asked a question that would forever change my life.

A group of young people from my church, myself included, went to hear Melody speak at a large gathering in Brighton. Melody and Keith both became believers in 1975 and immediately devoted their life to sharing with young people the message of surrendering everything to Christ. Keith and two of their children died in a plane crash in July 1982, but Melody had continued to lead their Last Days Ministries. Now here she was in England, challenging a group of us to the mission field. We watched a video of Keith singing and heard his passion as he talked about the millions of people who were lost without Christ. Melody threw out the challenge: "Who will stand up and go to the ends of the earth with the message of Jesus?"

Right there, in front of everyone, I stood up. I stood up because I

knew that Jesus was real; He had changed my life. I had dedicated my life to Him, and I believed He was there, calling me out.

I had no idea what this was going to mean in my life. Up until this point my only foray beyond British shores had been a day trip to France when I was ten. English to the core, I had no idea about life beyond our isles, although I watched the news regularly and was aware of world events—the Lebanese civil war, the Soviet invasion of Afghanistan, the Ethiopian famine, the apartheid controversy in South Africa, the increased attention to the AIDS epidemic. But it was a movie that helped me decide to leave the security of home.

I was an avid movie fan; I loved to go out with friends on a Friday night to see the latest film. So in 1984 when I entered the theater to see The Killing Fields, I expected to enjoy myself. The film—based on actual events that took place in Cambodia beginning in the 1970s—was shocking and tragic beyond belief. The Killing Fields portrays the agony of Cambodia under the insane, savage dictatorship of Pol Pot and the Khmer Rouge. I just couldn't believe that it was possible for people to undergo such suffering as I saw on the screen, that armed children younger than me took over a nation and slaughtered a third of the population. This had actually been happening on the other side of the world while I had been safe and comfortable at home.

I wanted to do my part to bring the Good News of Jesus Christ to a hurting world. But up until this point my global exposure had been next to nothing. I had no idea how the world would leave its mark on me.

4

AN ADVENTURER FOR CHRIST

Prisons, prostitution, street kids, refugee migration, endless
African wars, female circumcision, AIDS, poverty, homeless-
ness, population explosion—if we were living in a global
village, our streets would be filled with all of these.
                                    —From Gary's journal: May 2003

In the summer of 1986 I was beginning a new direction in my life. I knew it was time to leave Crawley, England, and I knew I would never be the same.

On July 4, my parents took me to Three Bridges railway station for the first leg of my journey. I waved good-bye to my family and boarded the train to London. Some friends said they doubted I would ever want to come back. I was twenty years old, and there was a world waiting to be discovered. This was what I had lived for, ever since looking out over the Plymouth Hoe, watching the ships come and go.

I had been accepted as part of a summer evangelism team heading to Austria with Operation Mobilization. We crossed the English Channel via ferry to Belgium, where our group joined students from all over the world at a camp headquartered in an old Allied World War II military base. We spent a week of intense training on how to share Christ and encourage Christians throughout Europe. As part of our preparation, we were divided into groups of six to ten people who were paired with various churches in the area. Each team had a variety of opportunities to share the gospel—in prisons, at the beach, in parks; through music, drama, and conversation.

One hot day during the conference I was sitting on the grass when an American Korean stopped to chat. I had never met a Korean before but had heard many amazing stories about the huge churches in Korea and their twenty-four-hour prayer meetings. Throughout the twentieth century the gospel has transformed Korea, and now its churches are sending missionaries with that same gospel message all across the world. The more days I spent at the conference, the more insecure I became about everything. Who was I that I could be involved in bringing the gospel to people who had never heard? I felt weak and intimidated.

But as we talked, my Korean friend quoted 2 Corinthians 12:9: "My grace is sufficient for you, for my power is made perfect in weakness." I didn't realize it at the time, but this passage would be an important verse in my life for years to come. No matter what happened in my life, through my failures and struggles, the Lord would always stand by me and be my strength in all my weaknesses. My Christian walk has been a constant struggle. Even after laying it all at the feet of Jesus, this follower of Christ still battles with sin, failure, and discouragement.

A Beautiful Desolation

At the end of the conference our team of ten students traveled to
Bruck, a small town in picture-postcard Austria, near the Hungarian
border. While western Austria is Alpine country, in the eastern part
of the country the rugged mountains give way to rolling hills, open
farmland, and beautiful, quiet villages. In the summer the roads are
clogged with slow-moving traffic because the farmers, driving in
open tractors, still enjoy a gentler pace of life. As we drove along,
my attention was drawn to statues of religious icons, mostly of
Mary, enshrined in little wooden houses, protecting the fields and
the harvest.

For the next two months my team was involved in various ministries in the nearby villages. In Bruck our team slept on the floor of 31
a local Baptist church and worked with its ten members. Ten! It was
the only church for miles around. Here I was in a country rich with
history and cultural treasures, abounding in natural beauty—yet
spiritually desolate.

I felt overwhelmed by the emptiness of so many people who
did not know the message of forgiveness in Christ. I had been
brought up in a culture where churches were plentiful and many
went to church. Here everyone claimed to be Catholic, but few
had any kind of relationship with Christ except by name. I was
weighed down with the fact that Europeans had such a rich religious history but had never heard His message. It was the first
time—but not the last—I realized that although people may have
heard the name of Christ, significantly fewer have ever heard His
teachings.

It was a shock to meet so many people who had never really
taken time to hear about the gospel. It was the first step that the
Lord was using to place His call on my life.

How, then, can they call on the one they have not believed in?
And how can they believe in the one of whom they have not
heard? And how can they hear without someone preaching to them?
And how can they preach unless they are sent? As it is written,
"How beautiful are the feet of those who bring good news!"
(Romans 10:14-15)

In Austria I experienced for the first time in my life the hostilities
between Catholics and evangelicals. How could this be? Why is it
that our two traditions worship the same Christ, and yet such
hatred, suspicion, and ignorance separate us? This is true everywhere. Often the Baptist church on one side of the road has little to
do with the Pentecostals on the other. It seems that in many cases,
the Christians are as guilty of this as those in all other religions and
multiethnic nations torn by factional strife.

These divisions in the church bothered me then and still do
today. It is bad enough that the church worldwide is experiencing
hostilities and persecution, but the resentment between denomina-
tions and the often deep schisms between believers can create
great discouragement.

Although I didn't know it at the time, one day I would sit with
Bonnie in Lebanon and listen over and over to the similar stories
of one group attacking another. I have learned that most preju-
dice comes from ignorance, from misunderstanding another
group's way of life and beliefs. However, the Bible says that God
so *loved* the world that *whoever* believes shall gain eternal life.
Jesus always seemed to have the ability to cross any social, eco-
nomic, ethnic, or religious line. It was true when He walked this
earth, and it is true today.

It is the Lord who is able to make a beautiful worldwide tapestry with all the diversity and differences in the church. We are His bride, His people.

The Voyage Begins

After my Austrian experience, I was ready to embark on another voyage—one that would last years and take me around the world. I was still intrigued by my memories of the MV Logos when it came to England three years before. I was drawn to the ship because it was dedicated to demonstrating and sharing the message of Jesus all around the world. I remember the amazement I felt as I boarded the ship and realized that Christians could do something so exciting. Even back then, I knew I wanted to join.

I flew for the first time out of London with a team of sixteen other OM volunteers. Destined for Mombasa, Kenya, we flew on the Russian airline Aeroflot bound first for Moscow—five years before the collapse of the Soviet bloc. The plane was cramped and noisy, and I was stuck in a window seat at the very back of the cabin next to a large and unpleasant-smelling person. The flight to Moscow took about five hours. As we approached the airport my face was glued to the window, but I could not see much because the huge engines on the tail obstructed my view. But I didn't mind at all—this was going to be a great adventure.

Upon landing in Moscow, we had to stand in line where we were inspected and questioned by a very scary man who thought he was important. When we met his approval, we were given the privilege of sitting in the airport for the next twelve hours. As we waited, I thought of all the missionaries and Christians who had suffered throughout the Soviet regime and all those who had smuggled Bibles through that very airport. Growing up I had read several missionary books that detailed unspeakable persecution such as Richard Wurmbrandt described in his book, *Tortured for Christ*. I thought of the warnings I had often heard as a child about possible attacks from the Communist world. I remembered how we would pray for the suffering church behind the Iron Curtain. All these memories made me more tense as I sat there waiting in the airport.

But the tension receded when we continued our flight to Mombasa, on Kenya's eastern coast, and finally beheld the MV *Doulos* gleaming white against the blue sky. This was it! When we got to the ship docked in the harbor, I was filled with excitement as we walked up its gangway. On board, I learned, were three hundred and fifty workers from over forty countries who served alongside volunteers from each country the ship visits. The ship held more than ten thousand different book titles on a wide range of subjects, from medicine to classic literature, in a variety of languages—although, as I would learn, people all over the world were eager to learn and read English. It was not uncommon to see thousands of people lining up for books at the places the ship docked. Teams traveled from the ship with local believers to schools, prisons, hospitals, and churches— wherever they could find the poorest of the poor.

Over the next several years I traveled with MV *Doulos* and MV *Logos II*, another OM ship, around Africa, Europe, and Asia. The entire adventure was formative in my spiritual journey, opening my eyes to the suffering and needs of humanity around the world. I think I was just shocked to see how much of the world lives in poverty, lacking the human rights we have come to expect in the West.

The Ivory Coast

In 1991, I had already been on the ships for several years when we visited the Ivory Coast in West Africa. Soon after arriving in Abidjan, we were invited to help with Prison Fellowship (an organization started by Chuck Colson who had been imprisoned himself because of his role in Watergate). This prison, like many I had seen, was overcrowded, filthy, and highly corrupt. The government wanted to clear out some of the prisoners, so fifteen hundred were being released.

They came out one at a time. First the women were released—many of them were wearing good clothes and makeup. I was told that they were healthier and in better condition than most prisoners because of prostitution. I did not know whether to feel sorry for them or angry with the system that used them.

Following the women were the men, hundreds of them, rail-thin and exhausted-looking. They smelled terrible, and I realized that inside the prison there were few, if any, showers or any place to get clean. I heard that, in some cases, there were so many men in one cell that it was difficult for them all to lie down to sleep.

Then, about fifty men who were mentally handicapped in varying degrees came out and wandered towards us. I was stung with how cruel the world can be. As they came out we gave them food and used several vans throughout the day to help them get home.

In the afternoon people were being carried out on stretchers. Many of these men had been injured in the prison. I carried a man in my arms to the back of the truck. He was coughing blood into a bag. He had a severe form of tuberculosis. I spent a little time talking with him and told him about Jesus as we drove him to the hospital.

When I brought him to the entrance of the hospital a doctor came and said, "He is homeless and we do not want him here. Take him back where you found him." I couldn't believe that he wouldn't help. The man was in a terrible state and this was his only hope. I pleaded for his life and waited for ages, knowing the van was needed to help others. Finally the doctor said he would take care of him. But the next day one of my friends visited the hospital and learned that the man had died in the night.

I have often thought about that man. He was a black, uneducated Muslim. He had nothing to call his own and no family. I was the last person you'd think God would use to fight for this man's life. There I was, from a privileged European background, educated and able to leave this nightmare any time; he had nothing, just poverty and sickness. He represents millions of people all over the world that I saw. The street children, the prostitutes, and the masses of poor.

I knew I could never help people out of their suffering, but I realized that the gospel is for the rich, the poor, and the suffering. God's love is for all people.

> I was sick, naked, in prison, in a filthy refugee camp, and you never came (see Matthew 25:42–44).

It was as if I was holding Jesus!

Moody Calls

A couple of Christian leaders told me I should really consider training for further ministry at a Bible school. *Bible school?* To me Bible schools exemplified the sort of know-it-all, establishment "churchiness" I continually struggled against. I had been blessed with some amazing experiences, hated being bored, and loved the adventure of living for Jesus and pursuing the life He challenged me to. I had met believers who had burned out during their college years. Bible school? GPAs? I felt I had received more schooling walking among the poor of Asia and Africa than I could if I were sitting in a stuffy classroom.

But after considerable prayer, it became clear that the Lord was indeed leading me to rejoin the world of academics. Ever eager for new worlds to explore, I looked to America for possibilities. I applied to three schools, but in my heart I knew God was calling me to Moody Bible Institute in Chicago. My hero, George Verwer, founder of Operation Mobilization, had gone there—and I knew the city was home to the Chicago Bears. I applied and was accepted at Moody. I couldn't wait to get there. I wanted to experience this American city, but I was unprepared for what the city had in store for me.

By this time it was mid-May 1991, and I was expected at the college by the first week in August. I had no money, no plane ticket, no visa. But I knew I would get to school. That summer I worked two jobs, sacrificing and scraping everything together so that I could go to Moody.

In August I found myself aboard a Northwest 747, flying from London to Chicago with a connection in Minnesota. I smiled to myself and thought, *Wow, this is America!* The sun was shining, and America looked so beautiful. Then I landed at O'Hare in Chicago. When I walked outside to the curb in the arrivals area I saw all the limousines. I couldn't believe it. I thought for sure there must be a lot of famous people here, all waiting to leave. I had never seen a limo before. A big Texan sporting a white Stetson stood there with his bags. I was overwhelmed—so those cowboy hats weren't just worn by J. R. Ewing on *Dallas*, the '80s TV soap about Texas's rich and powerful! I asked him about the limos and he said, "Son, those things come thicker than the fleas on the back of a dog." I laughed so hard. I could not have had a greater welcome to this new world called America. As I rode in the Moody van into the city, I couldn't believe how huge and beautiful Chicago looked. It seemed nothing was impossible.

Shortly after arriving on campus at MBI, the international students all met and were given a crash course on our new home. Moody is located just a few blocks from Lake Michigan and the shopping mecca of Michigan Avenue's Magnificent Mile. The lakefront skyline, dominated by the over-one-hundred-story John Hancock Building, forms a towering backdrop for the MBI campus. I had been all over the world, yet as I walked the streets of this city, I marveled at the power that seemed to emanate from the soaring buildings. I fell in love with Chicago—a romance that continues to this day.

Along with intense studies, life was challenging at Moody, as I made new friends, played soccer, and got involved in hands-on ministry.

For two years I was part of an evangelistic team that went out to Chicago's streets and parks to share the gospel. Sometimes we went down into the subways. The "L", as it is known in Chicago, is full of the rich and the poor, successful people and people we may consider failures. On the train I had many opportunities to sit and talk with people from all kinds of backgrounds.

There is a timelessness about sitting and waiting for the next train. In life, it seems we are always waiting for the next thing to take us to the next place. We always seem to be in a rush, looking for something to satisfy. Yet so much of what life offers only satisfies for such a short time.

I wrote this poem about a homeless fellow I met on the Chicago Blue Line train:

> Endless cold winter months,
> Ruthless temperatures plunder warmth
> Downward inside the timeless existence
> Of the Chicago subway.

The corridors' dirty gray-blue tiles and grimy floors,
Smells and dust, filth and waste,
Roar of steel on steel as trains thunder
Ever progressing to a new station.

Wind, blown, smashes through
As the unrelenting trains approach,
Thumping air through man-made caverns
Snake beneath the streets of Gold.

A whole civilization exists.
Oblivious is the casual traveler,
Unacquainted with the world below.

There a man I used to hear
Working a trumpet like an old friend.
Spectators haunted by the gravity of his pain
Revealed through the echoes of his heart
That bounced off the ceramic walls of his disturbing captivity.

A man who may have been cherished,
Who is nothing in the eyes of passersby,
Nowadays addicted to the tears of his life
Revealed in the notes of an old brass tool.

The sounds bounce
On the endless dirty walls
Into the universe of my mind.
They travel forever ringing as solitary anguish.

As there is nowhere in the subway
To hide from his beautiful terror,
So his loneliness has no place to rest.

Why does he play?
I cannot for one moment believe
He gets any more money than that for his alcohol
That wets his mouth as he plays the tunes of great men.
John Lennon can be heard revealed without words
Imagine all the lonely people.

What drives a man to surrender proudly
Without mercy to this place?
Perhaps this is the only way someone will listen.

We have all closed our ears.
We sit silently in neat lines rich and poor.
Sit waiting for the next train.
That unchanged monotonous train
Leading to the identical place.

An invisible optimism
A misplaced world
And we wrestle the graveled voice blowing,
Forced to meditate on the whimper of a trumpet.

5

A SOUL ON THE EDGE

Father, I want most of all to be completely surrendered to You. Lord, more than anything I need Your fellowship. . . . If there is something in my life that is keeping me from experiencing You in a deeper way, forgive me. I need You, Lord. Create in me a clean heart. Reveal to me even now where I need to change to be more like You!

—From Bonnie's journal

You might say a passion for Christ was in Bonnie's DNA.

Her ancestors on both sides were traditional Mennonites, ethnic Germans who lived and farmed in Russia and fled to Canada early in the twentieth century to escape the darkness that was beginning to fall over their vast homeland. Katherine Epp, one of Bonnie's great-grandmothers, bore sixteen children, six of whom preceded her in death. The story is that she spent her last day on this earth praying at length for the salvation of her children. One of those children, Henry, declared with his last breath, "Glory! Forever and ever!"

Henry's daughter, Ann, met Al Penner while working at Hartland Christian Camp near Sequoia National Forest in northern California—he was a counselor; she was a dining-room hostess. Both Ann and Al had come to the United States from Canada. Al's father, another Henry, was deeply involved in evangelistic ministries in Los Angeles. After they were married, Al and Ann settled near L.A., where Bonnie Denise Penner was born in 1971. Little Bonnie had just begun to walk when Al was transferred by Shell Oil to Vancouver, Washington, near the Oregon border.

Vancouver, for Bonnie, is where life and memories began, on an eight-acre farm on a hill, complete with a pond. Bonnie and her older sister, Cheryl, were set free in what seemed like paradise.

One Sunday morning after coming home from church, ten-year-old Bonnie asked her mother, "How do you know you are going to heaven?" Her mother told her that she knew she was going to heaven because she trusted in Jesus. She explained to Bonnie that Jesus had loved her so much that He had died on a cross and paid the penalty for all of her sins. "Do you want to tell Jesus that you're sorry for your sins and ask Him to save you?" Bonnie's mom asked. Bonnie said yes, and they went into the bedroom, kneeling together as Bonnie gave her young life to Christ.

When Bonnie and I were dating, she often entertained me with stories about her days growing up on a farm. Conspicuously lacking in the Penner family was that centerpiece of so many other households around the world—a television set. Al and Ann had sold their TV when they moved, telling their girls, "We'll give you something else. What do you want?" Cheryl asked for a horse. Bonnie, still young, was fascinated with Cheryl's horse and she thought she also might like a horse. Finally, the day came when Cheryl saddled up the horse, and Bonnie mounted him. She rode to the back of the pasture, her horse moving at a slow and easy gait, just right for a beginning rider. I can imagine Bonnie's confidence growing. But when the horse turned and faced the barn, he broke into a full gallop. Bonnie's parents could hear the pounding hoofbeats, along with Bonnie's screams. It had started to rain. As the horse approached the barn he suddenly stopped, lowered his head, and little Bonnie was thrown right into a pile of manure outside the barn. Wet and filthy, she yelled, "I hate horses! I will never, never ride a horse again!" With that she stomped into the house.

Bonnie was always a strong, spirited soul. She was willing to try anything and didn't like the feeling of being defeated.

So with the horse experience behind her, Bonnie decided to explore other options. She finally decided upon a trampoline. It was a good choice. She loved spending time on the trampoline, sometimes even studying or sleeping on it.

The farm on the hill was an idyllic setting for playing, roasting hot dogs and watching the stars, sledding across the frozen pond, crying over *Anne of Green Gables,* and wondering which of her friends might become, in Anne's words, a "kindred spirit."

People Need the Lord

When she was fourteen Bonnie, impelled by a zeal to put feet on her faith during the summer, joined Teen Missions International, an organization that trains and sends out tens of thousands of students all over the world to share their faith. She rose early one summer morning to prepare to leave with a busload of young people heading to boot camp on Merritt Island, Florida—more than 2,600 miles away. As she showered, she sang at the top of her lungs, "People need the Lord . . ." Her parents lay in bed listening and thinking, *There's our little missionary!*

Bonnie's dad, Al, still remembers the words she sang: "At the end of broken dreams, people need the Lord."

At boot camp, workers really did wear boots—which Bonnie proudly kept in her bedroom for years later to symbolize all God had taught her through that crucial summer. She and the other students trained in teamwork, negotiated obstacle courses, and developed skills in drama, evangelism, puppetry, and even construction. Living in tents, students formed close friendships. Leaders challenged them with Bible teaching. It was hard work, but I know Bonnie loved it. In fact, later she joined a team working in the United Kingdom at the London City Mission.

From that time on, she committed her life to learning about her Lord and sharing her faith in Him. Ironically, I lived only about twenty-five miles from London, but it was about that same time that I was flying off to serve on the ships.

Bonnie had a strong will and a warm heart as a teenager. Her willfulness often got her in trouble, but as soon as she felt a hint of guilt that she might have hurt someone, she would burst into tears and immediately find the person to make up. Her parents often said, "God has given Bonnie this will so that one day it can be channeled into serving the Lord."

And so it was.

Wrestling with God

After graduation from high school Bonnie enrolled in Bodenseehof Bible School in southern Germany, which proved to be a time of growth and learning for her. One of her cousins had attended Moody Bible Institute in Chicago, and she encouraged Bonnie to apply. So in 1992, Bonnie headed east to what would become *her* school and *her* city.

It would be easy, particularly now that she is with the Lord, to paint a portrait of Bonnie as one of those "perfect Christian students" who never doubted, always succeeded, and effortlessly climbed the ladder of Christian service. Christian colleges are full of driven young men and women trying to achieve these goals (or marry someone trying to achieve these goals). Yet the reality was far more complex . . . and far more interesting. During our college years we both experienced great lows.

At Moody, Bonnie was required to do a summer of ministry. Her time with Teen Missions had been such a critical part of her past that she wanted to be stretched even more. She chose to go some- where tough and challenging: the Philippines. Her team leader for the trip was Andrea Arzikakis, a good friend who would eventually become Bonnie's mentor. Andrea always said Bonnie was like a refreshing can of soda shaken up and quickly opened. Her joy and exuberance sprayed all over the place. (Bonnie was hardly an emotionally inconspicuous person.) She also wasn't someone who needed to take a long time to think through decisions.

Bonnie had requested a rural and rustic area; she wanted a pioneer experience, the toughest placement. Andrea recognized Bonnie's zeal and honored her request. The place where she was housed was everything she wanted *and less* as far as accommodations were concerned! There was no running water (which meant no flush toilets), one cracked mirror, lots of geckos and rats, food she had a tough time stomaching, and a bed she had to share with one or two other young women. But I'm jumping ahead of the story.

You see, when Bonnie arrived in the Philippines, her exuberance for God had gone flat. Weeks prior to arriving in the Philippines,

Bonnie felt that she had completely lost her faith and no longer believed in God.

Her confession came out the second day of an extensive three-day cross-cultural training session. Andrea was conducting the sessions and noticed Bonnie was glaring at her. During one of the breaks Andrea approached her to ask what was up. Bonnie's response was unforgettable; she looked at Andrea and said, "I hate you." One of the good things about Bonnie was that you seldom had to guess where you stood with her. She was invariably up front, which made discernment a lot easier! Andrea thanked her for her candor and during a longer break asked if they could run some errands together. As they were out and about, Andrea asked

Bonnie to tell her more about why she hated her. Bonnie said that she hated Andrea because Andrea loved God.

Well, it didn't take a brain surgeon to realize that Bonnie had a dilemma; it would be difficult to evangelize for a God she didn't believe in and worse yet, *didn't like*. Andrea asked her to not go out to the field until they could sort things out. As they spent more time together, sorting things out metamorphosed into one of the most beautiful gifts for both Bonnie and Andrea.

Bonnie figured she had nothing to lose. She was in a foreign land with someone whom she thought she'd know only for the duration of her six-week trip, so she opened up.

Speaking from her heart, Bonnie explained that shortly after applying for the trip, she had prayed a very specific prayer requesting a specific gift. Because she wanted it so badly, she told God if she didn't get it she wouldn't believe in Him. She thought she could strong-arm God, but to her horror not only did she not receive what she wanted, but she also found herself unable to express her belief in Him. But God, in His infinite love, was not going to allow

Bonnie's faith to be built on this "If you'll give me, I'll give you . . ." attitude. Rather than answering a request that would lead to a continual cycle of doubt and difficulty, He answered the prayer in a way that would reveal to her who He was. In His love He allowed Bonnie's disbelief to take full rein.

Because Bonnie had been able to raise her support so quickly, she felt obligated to carry out her plan to serve in the Philippines, even though she had hit a crisis of faith. After the other missionaries were placed in their assignments, Bonnie and Andrea began a series of long discussions. Andrea recognized that the first challenge was figuring out how Bonnie could be reconnected with a God she said she no longer believed in. It seemed an insurmountable obstacle at the time: How do you pray to a God you don't believe in?

Andrea had been attending a local church with a dynamic pastor, and she persuaded Bonnie to meet with her and the pastor. At the end of the session, the pastor spoke of the enormous power of words and asked Bonnie, "Do you want to renounce the vow you made against God?" Bonnie said she would, but she didn't really expect anything to happen. Andrea had no idea what to expect but prayed to God that something would happen.

And it did. After renouncing the vow out loud, Bonnie experienced an immediate gift of faith that was firmly rooted in the living God. Both Bonnie and Andrea were caught off guard. Neither one of them anticipated such a complete and instantaneous result. Immediately, with tears streaming down her face, Bonnie asked God for forgiveness and was granted His unconditional acceptance. Then this wise pastor prayed that the places that previously stored words of death would house words of life and faith. Leaving the church, Bonnie seemed to be gliding on air. She was alive again, singing and laughing and proclaiming the reality of a loving God.

For Bonnie, faith in Christ had to be 100 percent real. She did not like pretentious Christianity and needed to know and experience God personally. It was a tension the two of us had in common. That summer Andrea baptized Bonnie. Her summer in the Philippines was a memory she always deeply cherished and shared with friends. It was her faith that motivated her to go and tell others about Jesus.

I wish I could tell you that after Bonnie confessed her struggles that she never again encountered difficulties in those arenas, but that would be a lie. Throughout the remainder of her life she continued to experience difficulties, but their power was diminished, while her faith was strengthened. She knew that her God was with her. She knew that He was strong. She knew that she could depend on Him. And she knew that even when she blew it, He was gracious and forgiving. She staked her life on these realities . . . and she unashamedly shared these realities with others.

6

THE OREGON TRAIL

*What is my purpose on earth? Our purpose is to glorify
God. In John 17:4 Jesus says, "I have brought you glory
on earth by completing the work you [called me and]
gave me to do." To fulfill our mission and purpose in life
we must do what He asks. But the only way to know
that is to surrender our will to Him.*
    —From Bonnie's journal: September 12, 1998

I could hardly believe what we were doing.

Bonnie and I had only been engaged a few days, and here we
were on a train, sadly watching the familiar Chicago skyline, like a
majestic friend, recede to the east. We were leaving the great city,
the lake, the buildings, the school, our friends—leaving everything
for Portland, Oregon. Bonnie fought off the tears quietly as the
screeching wheels wound through the suburbs sprawling to the
west. We had no money and few possessions, mostly books
packed up in apple boxes.

We both loved the great city of Chicago and were reluctant to leave, yet we both knew it was time to take our next steps. We were leaving one life and walking into another. A few years later we would again box everything up and leave what we loved for the unknown. It can be one of the painful prices to pay for those who feel called to go and serve wherever God directs.

But we were young. I had never seen the West Coast, and as the train rolled across the prairie, our spirits rose. We were in the last coach and could see the length of the glistening steel train as it snaked around curves, across the immense plains, and over land locked deep in winter; before the train climbed through the Rockies, blasting its horn at every junction. As I watched out the window, it appeared to me that little had changed since the earliest days of steam, when immigrants had carved and blasted their way through mountain passes. Our train wound through stunning gorges sparkling with snow and icy rivers, through mountains and evergreen forests.

We stopped in Salt Lake City, where a couple of years earlier a group of us from Moody had gone to learn about Mormonism and talk to people about what Jesus really taught. I found the people to be friendly as we shared the gospel, going door-to-door just as the Mormons do. We stood on one woman's doorstep talking about what she called the "burning in the bosom" as a way to know God is really in your life. As we were leaving, three police cars came speeding down the street, lights flashing. The officers rushed up to us and I asked, "What's the problem?" As I explained our work, one officer replied, "We are all Christians around here. You better leave now or we will arrest you."

We left quietly because I was on a student visa and did not want to tangle with the law. But I remember thinking it ironic that there was no real freedom for evangelicals to speak about Jesus in Utah. Although Mormons have many teachings similar to Christianity, they believe Jesus Christ is simply "a god," whereas the Bible clearly proclaims one God.

For Bonnie and me, it was a long ride to the coast, sleeping two nights in coach. I spent much of the time looking out the window, reflecting on all the places I had seen and what this latest adventure might promise. Bonnie, unfortunately, came down with the flu so that much of her journey was uncomfortable. Late in the afternoon the train slowly skirted the Columbia Gorge and pulled into Portland, where her sister, Cheryl, and Cheryl's future husband, Jason, picked us up. A new world was waiting to become our home.

And So We Were Married

Bonnie and I were married in April 1997.

All weddings have a dreamlike quality, seemingly suspended in time. What I most recall about that day is first, being terrified and second, watching a beautiful girl walk toward me, radiant in white, those eyes fixed on me. I knew that under Christ, two people were coming together, each of us bringing our best and our worst, all of it cloaked with His grace.

Most people fondly remember their first home as newlyweds. For Bonnie and me, it was an apartment in Portland surrounded by trees that would whisper in the soft Oregon breeze. Our front room had a vaulted ceiling and at a certain time of the day it would be filled with bright sunlight. Bonnie discovered petunias grew well in the climate and placed pots of them all over our dark-green deck.

In the evenings we would read, drink coffee, and play Scrabble. Our lives were quiet, disturbed only by the lady next door who would shriek during Sunday NFL games. Soon I was serving as a pastor to college-age students in a local church.

We needed income, so Bonnie and I applied for jobs at a bank. There were openings in the collections department which paid more. It wouldn't take long for us to realize why.

In the collections department, things were stressful. We had moved from a Bible college environment straight into dealing with other people's problems with money. We had to call people who had not paid bills. I heard every excuse imaginable. The guy in the booth next to me was nicknamed "the angry man": he just lost it with people who weren't paying their bills. I could understand his reaction, in a way, even though I had been taught that the customer is always right. I dealt with people who were in tens of thousands of dollars of debt. It wasn't always their fault—suddenly there's a medical emergency or a job is lost, and there's no money to pay the Visa bill.

Seeing the misery debt brings taught me lasting lessons about financial stability. Bonnie and I would come home emotionally drained from listening to people's problems. After close to four years on that job, I concluded that credit-card debt has become one of the most destructive elements in American society by enslaving people with monthly payments. I would speak to thousands over the years who rarely enjoyed an entire paycheck.

One Valentine's Day, we drove to the coast and found a cabin on the beach for the night. There we read together James Joyce's short story "The Dead," from *Dubliners*. The story describes people caught in lives of inconsequential living and dying. At the end, husband Gabriel looks over at his aging wife, who had had a lover in her teens. Deep down she had kept the lover's love locked up in her heart, and Gabriel realized that their relationship, for the most part, was passionless. Gabriel thought to himself, "Better pass boldly into that other world, in the full glory of some passion, than fade and wither dismally with age."

When we read that line, Bonnie and I looked at each other. We felt the same way! That was what we wanted for ourselves. We felt powerfully led to invest our lives well. In Philippians 3, Paul speaks of taking hold of that for which Christ has taken hold of you. We did not want to "wither dismally," poking along in dead-end jobs, never questioning our purpose in life. We knew that God had more for us to do. We felt like we were waiting on what adventure the Lord might have for us. But while we were waiting, we learned a lot about each other, about God, and about marriage.

"What Do You Want to Do with Your Life?"

Three years passed and we were still in Portland. We were now supervisors at the bank. I was struggling because I felt I was not living up to my potential—I had traveled the world, and here I was, still stuck in a cubicle, dealing with other people's debts.

Thinking the least I could do was earn a better paycheck, I applied for a promotion. I knew they liked my work; I figured I had a good shot at advancement. Before the interview I went shopping with Bonnie and bought a smart dark-blue suit with a tie to match so that when I had the interview I looked like a banker.

The day came. In the room where I was sitting, I noticed motes of dust floating in the shafts of sunlight that filtered through the blinds. I had a good relationship with the three men who conducted the interview. I answered the typical questions such as "What was the last book you read?" I knew the interview was going well, and then Mike, my manager, looked me squarely in the face and asked, "What do you want to do with your life?"

It was a crossroads moment. I knew that if I answered, "Mike, I want to make this company successful and make you look good," I would have aced the interview. Instead, hearing my heart and knowing it was over, I said, "I want to be a missionary and tell people around the world about Jesus." *Boom*, just like that, it was done.

I knew it was just a matter of time before I quit. I wanted to be climbing mountains or trekking through the jungle. I wanted to tell people about Jesus. I did not want to look up one day and find myself sitting in some corner office wondering where the years had gone. I did not want to wither. And neither did my beautiful Bonnie.

We still wanted to serve on the ships with OM, so we applied— but after a short wait, we received an e-mail informing us there was no room. I was crushed, and Bonnie was confused. Why would God lead us this way, if only to close the door?

In a time of prayer one day, the Lord spoke to Bonnie in a powerful way. She distinctly felt the Lord saying, *I have not called you to a place; I have called you to Myself.*

We realized that the point, then, was not us and our wonderful, selfless serving and doing for Jesus. We were striving and struggling, like Martha in the Bible, to be always doing something for God. Yet all through the Bible the Lord was calling us to love Him, to be close to Him, to listen to Him—to stop running around and instead pay attention to Him.

So we let go of our dream of serving on the ships, at least for then. But what did God have for us next?

The answer came in a most unexpected way.

7

EAT SAND!

The past six months have seemed like a whirlwind of change. At one point we were going on the ships; now we're not. We are now considering going to the Arabian Peninsula. There seem to be a lot of options for us there—teaching English, working with tourism, or just learning Arabic. I don't know what God has for us, but I want to be available to go. . . . I feel like God has me blindfolded and is leading me along a path I don't quite understand. But I will follow Him.

—From Bonnie's journal: April 17, 2000

Bonnie and I had reached a crisis point in our lives, not knowing where the Lord was leading us next, not sure what He wanted us to do in order to serve Him best. I e-mailed Mike Hack, a friend and mentor from my days on the ships. "I don't understand what God is doing in my life," I told him. "I've been on the ships; I've been trained; I've gone through Bible college; and I can't even seem to get a job within the organization I want to work for."

Mike replied with one sentence. "Go to the Middle East and eat sand. Love, Mike."

Not, "Oh, Gary, I'm so sorry for you." He didn't care that I was struggling here in the States; he simply said, "Go and humble yourself. Forget about trying to find some glamorous position. Eat humble pie. Eat sand."

Early on in our discussions, Bonnie and I had both pretty much ruled out the Middle East. We didn't want to have anything to do with the conflicts, the danger, the Islamic culture. Perhaps we were poisoned by the constant negative impressions we saw and heard in the media. We each read Mike's e-mail separately, and independently we both felt it was God speaking to us. Yet we both were also thinking about the other's reaction. I knew that God was speaking to me, but I was sure Bonnie was never going to want to go. Likewise, Bonnie was feeling drawn to the Middle East as well, but didn't know if she could ever convince me to go. So we each kept it a secret. Finally, the next day, Bonnie asked, "Did you read Mike's e-mail?" I looked at her and I could see it written all over her face. We were thinking the same thing: God wanted us in the Middle East.

We began looking at countries on the Persian Gulf, but we learned that in many of those countries Bonnie would have to wear black and be veiled. I was not prepared for my beautiful wife to be all covered up. Then I heard about Lebanon. Friends told me, "There you can be what you want to be. It's a beautiful place—it has mountains, skiing, and is very fertile because of the Mediterranean climate. And there are Christians there."

It became clear to us that God was sending us to take a message of hope and love to a war-torn nation on the other side of the world. Not too much time passed before we put price tags on everything in our beloved little apartment in the trees and invited our friends to a house sale. For four years this had been our safe and quiet retreat, our first home together. Now we were selling the bookshelves we had built together, the pine dining table, the cherished little things we had acquired over time. That night, seeing the home she had put together over the years so quickly disassembled, Bonnie wept quietly. When we lay down in our bed for the last time, the apartment looked very white and very empty. Bonnie said to me that night, "It's not that I am not excited and don't want to go, it is just that it is hard to leave our home here." I understood completely.

We spent time with Bonnie's family, and then flew to London to be with my family for a couple of weeks. Over the 2001 New Year's holiday we took a train across Europe to visit our good friends, Matt and Melinda Edwards, in Hungary. Matt had been my best man and was now leading worship at Calvary Chapel in Budapest.

On this New Year's, as we watched the fireworks, we celebrated a new century (according to some) and a new era in our lives. I was excited about all the possibilities about to unfold in the coming year.

Go

I don't want to give the impression that our decision to move to the Middle East for a two-year stint was understood by the people in our lives. It wasn't. When we told our friends, many of them could not believe what we were doing. But it was our love for Jesus that drove us to let go of what normal life could offer. We had counted the cost and knew the dangers. We felt that Jesus lived in the same way, with few possessions, no home, and an itinerary that took Him to places where people would possibly want to kill Him.

He demonstrated love. Would Bonnie and I be able to do the same? We wanted to find out.

Did we feel a particular burden for the Middle East, for Muslims? Not really. I leave fuzzy feelings to people like the Mormon woman I met in Salt Lake City, the one who got the "burning in the bosom." I've seen too many people with "burdens" go overseas with warm fuzzy ideals and then a year later they become disillusioned and return home. No, the Bible simply says, "Go." It doesn't say, "Wait for a sense of calling." Certainly I believe that people are called—but, more important, we go because God tells us to go, not because we *feel* like going. Calling is more than feelings.

In fact, it's easy to romanticize the missionary life. But the reality is altogether different. It means giving up everything: your language, your car, your friends, your family; it means giving up Wal-Mart and Walgreens and clean streets and safety and working electricity. It means you might be going into a war zone; you might be jailed; you might be kicked out of the country for trying to plant an underground church.

And it isn't always heroic. You go to a country where no one cares about you, no one is interested in you. You feel almost silly walking around the streets trying out the new words in the new language you've learned: "I like my blue cup." There is a certain amount of frustration because it takes time before you can interact deeply in conversation with the people you are trying to reach because of the language barrier. You know they're looking at you and talking about you, but you can't understand what they're saying. You feel isolated because you might be one of only a few foreigners in a city of three hundred thousand people. And sometimes you must live off the support of friends and churches, whereas if you'd stayed at home you could be self-sufficient, making a good living.

Bonnie and I realized what every missionary must realize: *You have to die to yourself.* You have to be willing to say over and over, "Yes, Lord. Any time, any place, whatever you want, including dying." He says, *Go.* And we go.

War, Peace, and Change

Over the months prior to leaving, we spoke with many churches and friends who might be interested in partnering with us in prayer and finances. It took months of hard preparation. But then, one day we were ready. We flew off to a country we knew next to nothing about—but would come to love.

I had met many Arabs over the years, but all I knew of Lebanon came from TV images of the recent civil war (1975–1990). Lebanon had once been a relatively stable, Western-oriented country, governed by a coalition of Muslims and Maronite Christians (a Catholic sect). This fragile balance maintained civility until the early 1970s, as the Muslim population grew and eclipsed the Christian population, and Muslims became increasingly dissatisfied with the political arrangement that kept Christians in power. Adding to the volatility of the situation was the influx of Palestinians into southern Lebanon. The simmering feuds finally boiled over when the "Christian party" attacked a busload of Palestinian terrorists in April 1975. In 1976, neighboring Syria joined the war, sent in troops, and occupied parts of the country. Lebanon was also caught in the crossfire of Israeli–PLO conflicts. In 1982 the Israeli army marched up to Beirut, pushed the PLO out, and occupied southern Lebanon for nearly two decades.

Muslims have now become the dominant political, religious, and cultural force in Lebanon. Thousands of Christians have fled and continue to flee. Southern Lebanon, where we were heading, was and is volatile. Yet we knew that was where we needed to be.

We flew out of London to Beirut by way of Prague. We were excited and yet afraid; we had no idea what to expect from this little country struggling with the aftermath of war. We had been invited to serve with two churches in Sidon, the third-largest city in Lebanon, located about fifty miles from the Israeli border. The events of September 11 were still months away, but Lebanon was technically at war with Israel, and there was a lot of animosity toward the U.S. government. I wondered how people would respond to us.

By the time the plane came swooping in over the Mediterranean Sea and onto the runway, it was already early in the morning. As the plane touched down, all the Lebanese travelers on board clapped. Bonnie was so excited, she started giggling and clapping with the others. It all was quite exciting for both of us. Finally we had arrived. We were prepared to do something worth living for.

Our first impression was of a lovely land of mountains bordered by the sea. Beirut sits at the base of a mountain that sparkles with the yellow-white lights of the city as far as the eye can see.

Our host greeted us at the airport and drove us south to Sidon in his old Toyota van. He told us a little about his life—how he had lived through the war years in Beirut repairing people's houses and preaching the gospel until now. The freeway in Lebanon, the autostrade, follows the coastline which is stunning at sunset. It's also extremely dangerous. All along our route, the guardrails were mangled—evidence of Lebanon's high accident rate, which I had heard about and which I was to experience firsthand. On our first night in the country I noticed many of the vehicles were driving without lights. Cars cut us off as they sped around the corners and seemed unable to stay within the white lines.

But we arrived safely and dragged our bags up the four flights of stairs into our hosts' apartment, where everyone was still sleeping. In the darkness we slipped into bed. I was surprised just how cold everything was in this Mediterranean midwinter—cold enough to need heaters.

So there we lay in a strange bed, feeling at once displaced and expectant. We were so excited, we weren't sure we could sleep. But after such a long trip, we were both exhausted, and we quickly drifted into deep slumber. We woke early and joined the family for a breakfast of *kibbis* (Arab bread) with sliced tomatoes and sour cream. Just like that, our world had completely changed—and we had to adjust. It was not going to be easy.

Faith and Fear

We were assigned to Sidon, an ancient and strategic port city and trading center in Phoenician times, to work alongside two long-established churches. Up in the hills is a small Baptist church in the Catholic-controlled village of Mieh Mieh; and down in the city proper was a Christian and Missionary Alliance (CMA) church.

In the first weeks, we began full-time Arabic lessons. In the morning we'd spend a few hours in classes and in the afternoon we walked around Sidon and met people while practicing our new words. This intense language study would be part of our daily routine over the next two years. We tried to develop vocabulary that was immediately relevant. But it was tough. One neighbor always asked me the same question every time I passed his house. I could never answer him because I couldn't understand his accent and didn't know what he was saying. Finally, one day as I passed by, he said in Arabic, "How are you? Where are you going?" I understood him! And I was able to answer him. Although the language was hard, the effort was definitely worth it. As we began to understand the people, we also began to feel closer to them.

Neighbors Old and New

Aside from learning Arabic, we also needed to find a place to live. In a place where even walking out onto the street was an event, finding an apartment seemed a daunting task. Bonnie, especially, was tired of staying in other people's homes and longed to have one she could make our own.

We looked at many places, finally finding a spacious three-bedroom unit on the seventh floor of an apartment building over-looking the Mediterranean Sea. The apartment had an amazing view of the famous Sea Castle, a Crusader fortress built by Richard the Lionhearted in the thirteenth century. It had marble floors, textured walls, sliding glass windows, and a balcony that would become a favorite place for us to watch the sunset—and it was only two hundred and fifty dollars a month. God had provided for us beyond our expectations! This place would be a haven for Bonnie and me, as well as a place we could use to share hospitality with the people we would come to love.

Lebanon, with its strategic location on the Mediterranean, the aquatic artery of the ancient world, has seen Persians, Romans, and Ottoman Turks invade at various times in its history. Biblical connections abound, including the temple of Eshmun, which was located only two miles from our home. This ancient temple to Baal is where King Ethbaal terrorized this part of the world and where his daughter Jezebel became a princess and priestess of the temple. Amid the ruins of the site, in a graphic depiction of the religious history of the area, is the mosaic floor of a Byzantine church. Through the middle of the temple ruins is a road lined with broken pillars, reminding the visitor of the glory that once was.

Just to the north of Sidon is a beachhead called *Ras el Nabi Younes*—"the headland of the prophet Jonah." Here, tradition says, the whale spat the disobedient prophet out on dry land. And just south of Sidon, on the way to Tyre (Sour), is the little town of Sarafand, or Zarabeth, where Elijah ate the last meal of the widow. As I looked around at our new home, I could imagine Elijah walking these same streets and hills, wondering how he would stand against the false god Baal. In Sidon's Old City a church where the apostle Paul stayed (Acts 27:3) is still standing. The room has remained unchanged over two millennia, and few know it exists.

Our street, Riad Asolah, was named after one of the prewar Lebanese presidents. The street was the main artery for Syrian tanks rolling through from the north in 1976 and Israeli tanks rumbling in from the south in 1982. Even today the very wealthy live close to the very poor. Two decades of war destroyed much of the country's infrastructure, so that simple communication—things we in the West take for granted—is a major challenge. Cellular telephones make it easier, but cost about forty dollars a month—a high price to pay in a country where the average wage is between two hundred and five hundred dollars a month.

Once we moved into our apartment, we found that our electricity operated on a four-hours-on, four-hours-off schedule. We realized very quickly the importance of not being in the elevator when the electricity turned off!

Gradually we became acquainted with our neighborhood. A tire dealer was located just below our apartment. The owners, a Palestinian family, worked long hours in the shop. We became great friends, and I spent a lot of time with the grandfather, who was wonderfully kind. We talked about life, and he enjoyed that I practiced my Arabic with him. Next door to us was *Maktabe Ziad*—"Ziad's bookshop." Bonnie and I spent hours in there practicing Arabic. The first day I saw the owner, Ziad, he grasped my face with his two large hands and pulled me toward him. He kissed both cheeks and, laughing, said, *"Wij tieben,"* which means, "You have a delicious face."

If you kept going down the street, you would come to a *doucan*—corner shop. These are all over, supplying the neighborhoods with their groceries. I loved to stop by the doucan and visit with the owner, Fouad. He knew everyone and greeted everyone who walked into his shop by name. *I want to have that same connection to the people,* I thought. *Over time, as I become more fluent in the language, I will.* Fouad, too, was a kind soul, always offering me his strong Arabic coffee. We often sat and talked about the state of the world. As we became friends, I learned that Fouad had a great respect for Christians. He often expressed his longing for peace in his nation.

Across the road and next to the flower shop you'd find the Internet café. Home Internet access is expensive in Lebanon, so Internet cafés are popular. There, twenty PCs were always humming as kids played computer games or surfed the Internet. Down the street and closer to downtown was my favorite "fast food" shop, El Baba. Like many other vendors, El Baba sold the Lebanese version of fast food, *shwarma*—lamb, beef, or chicken cooked on a spit and then wrapped in flat bread. Often these vendors set up shop right on the sidewalk. The fragrance is enticing, and in the evenings men congregate to have a sandwich. It didn't take long for Bonnie and me to realize how much we loved Lebanese food. I've eaten all over the world and have never found such unique cuisine, influenced by so many countries.

Slowly we began to get to know the local Christians in Sidon. Both of the local churches had been attacked and controlled by Islamic militia during the civil war, sparking a mass exodus of Christians to the West. There are larger populations of Christians from Beirut northwards, but it seemed there were very few Christians in the south. There were even fewer foreigners.

Today the typical evangelical church in Lebanon might have thirty or forty in attendance, sometimes more. Usually the congregation is made up of fairly conservative, deeply committed, and faithful Christians. These churches do see people making commitments to the Lord, and although Lebanon does enjoy religious freedom under its constitution, increasingly Lebanese Christians live in fear of Islam. Believers tend to huddle in their enclaves rather than interacting with Muslims.

Not long after we arrived in Lebanon I was talking to our pastor, who lived in a Christian community, "The Church really needs to be sharing more with Muslims," I challenged him.

"It's just not that easy," the pastor softly said. "We just went through a civil war killing each other. You can't come into our world with ideals and expect us to change."

As I began to learn about life in the Middle East I discovered that what many Christians are most afraid of is militant Islam. Yet I learned about fifteen million Arabs call themselves Christian in one form or another, throughout the Middle East. But many have become isolated and passive in response to Islamic aggression. One question kept coming to mind: "Do they not have a right to exist and practice their faith—especially in Lebanon where there is supposed to be freedom of religion?"

A Call to Listen

When we first arrived, Bonnie and I spent a lot of time learning Arabic together and trying to get to know the people. Bonnie noted our first weeks in her journal:

> *I feel like a little kid again, trying to learn this language. I only know five words or so, and these are the only words I say. I think people must really laugh at me. I feel a little strange being here because I don't feel like I have a purpose. I almost feel I should be out "evangelizing" or something . . . I was really feeling down about it when I felt God saying to me, "Bonnie, all I want and expect from you is your availability and willingness to be used wherever I have you."*

It became apparent that ministering in this part of the world is different—less organized, less "official." It has to be, due to the restrictions of sharing the gospel in a Muslim culture. But as time went on and we began to feel more at home in Lebanon, we learned something I'm not sure we understood before: Muslims are, first of all, people like us—people who sleep, laugh, cry, eat, pay bills, work, have kids. The images we had seen on the news of angry protests are only part of the story. We got to know our neighbors; some wealthy but mostly the poor. I got to know the kids who played soccer on the local fields while Bonnie began making friends with some of the women around the neighborhood. We saw how they enjoyed honest, lively dialogue, were interested in finding out what followers of Christ believe, and earnestly sought common ground. Arabs appreciate leisurely conversation, eating and drinking coffee together, and a slower pace of life than we in the West are used to. I realized that the only way Muslims and Christians could ever find peace with each other would be through thoughtful dialogue and understanding. I was secure in my beliefs as a Christian, but I needed to learn everything I could about Islam, especially studying the Qur'an, and becoming more and more fluent in the beautiful Arabic language.

Dialogue is not polemics, which says, "You are wrong and we are right and you need to repent." Yes, there's a place for that, but I quickly found that I wasn't going to win many Muslims to Christ with that attitude. Dialogue is not apologetics, which says, "This is what we believe; now tell me what you believe. That's great for you; this is great for me." Rather, true dialogue asks questions: what do you believe about Jesus? about God? What do you believe about creation? about sin? I quickly learned I could understand a lot about God and life through discussions with my Muslim friends. Dialogue does not attack or try to convert. Instead, it listens and learns, and it makes deep friends. I had so much to learn in two years. But I knew that's what my priority needed to be.

> Now we see things imperfectly as in a cloudy mirror, but then we will see everything with perfect clarity. All that I know now is partial and incomplete, but then I will know everything completely, just as God now knows me completely. (1 Corinthians 13:12, NLT)

We knew that as followers of Christ, we had the Truth—and we were grateful for the privilege to share it respectfully and humbly. As Bonnie and I settled into our new home, sharing the Truth began with simple conversations.

As we met our neighbors, we talked often about the man who

taught us to forgive our enemies, help our neighbors, and love the unlovely. We shared the message of Jesus—the same message that compels Christians to go to the refugee camps, to the street kids, and to the prostitutes of the world—not to convert them to some boring "religion," but to give them *hope*. It was this same Jesus who had walked through the region of Sidon two thousand years ago.

8

LOVE IN A TIME OF WAR

Lord, here we are in the Middle East. How many people will die in this city of Sidon today without knowing You? How can I worry about my life or Gary's life when tens of thousands of people may die and face eternal damnation today? Lord, my life is already hidden with You. I know You. I have the truth. There is nothing they can take from me!

—From Bonnie's journal

"Normal" in Lebanon, we quickly learned, was not like "normal" in the U.S. or the U.K. On the one hand, people went to work, bought groceries, watched TV—just like anywhere. On the other hand, things happened. . . .

One day a Piper plane flew past our apartment. I took notice because up until that point the only planes I had ever seen were Israeli military jets. Bonnie and I were studying at our dining room table with our Arabic teacher. I looked out of our apartment window and, clearly visible from our seventh-floor apartment, was a little plane flying over the beach. I wondered what the pilot was doing. It took our teacher by surprise, too, but we continued to study. After the lesson was finished we ate and listened to the BBC over our shortwave radio. There it was, one of the headline stories: "Piper plane shot down over northern Israel when the pilot ignored demands by Israeli helicopters to turn around."

I was shocked; I had just been looking at the very same pilot. What had he been thinking? Lebanon and Israel had been in a constant state of war. Much of the conversation of my friends in southern Lebanon revolved around a desire for revenge, or the celebration of any defeat of a perceived enemy. Later some suggested the pilot had lost his mind. But for me it was a rude awakening. I realized then just how much hostility resided between the two countries.

It became almost a weekly occurrence to hear or see the Israeli jets fly over Sidon. Some said it was to let the Lebanese know they were there. One night when it was already dark, we suddenly heard antiaircraft fire going up with tracers all around the city. It continued for quite some time and we really didn't know what to think. This was so unlike the peaceful lives we had had before coming to Lebanon.

It was our goal not to get involved politically with all that was going on. But almost every day people would ask us what we thought of this politician or that war. It was hard to have a conversation that was not politically motivated or turned the discussion to the evils of Israel. This intense hatred made us often feel lonely. We had not suffered the things that these people had suffered. I soon realized we needed lots of compassion for them that we didn't possess ourselves.

"Hezbollah Number One!"

Late one night, Bonnie and I were returning from a night out in Beirut, Lebanon's capital, which is about forty-five minutes from Sidon. We had gone to see a movie and it was about 10:30 p.m. Since we didn't have a car at that point, we flagged down a taxi to take us to the street where we would catch our bus back to Sidon. We jumped into the backseat and noticed another passenger sitting in the front with the driver. Speaking the little Arabic I knew, I asked to be dropped off at the bus depot. The driver agreed. The battered Mercedes wound its way through the badly lit, pothole-ridden streets, slowly ambling its way through the traffic to the Shiite area. We were driving down an unlit street when the man in the passenger seat turned around and loudly yelled with a big smile, "Hezbollah number one!" Hezbollah, of course, is the feared organization in Lebanon. Bonnie and I sat frozen, thinking, *They could take us anywhere.* But I smiled back and yelled, "Hezbollah number one!"

This seemed to satisfy the two unshaven men. Meanwhile, Bonnie and I prayed intensely and were relieved when the cab dropped us off on the correct street. We may have had nothing to fear from these men. But even though they seemed to be kind, their connection to the terrorism movement scared us. I discovered that fear most often set in when I did not understand the situation. In order to allay that fear, I promised myself I would study as much as possible the history of the region.

Another time I was riding through a poorer section of Beirut. I looked out and saw two little boys in an alley, illuminated by hazy orange sunshine. One was wearing an oversized white vest, dirty and dragging on the ground. They were play-fighting with sticks and laughing, unaware of their poverty, lost in the images they had grown up with. As I watched the boys, I was struck by the fact that for them, fighting was simply a way of life and they had learned their survival skills early. They had to. These were the children of war. They saw the fighter jets streak across the skies; they climbed through the rubble of conflict every day. It was all they knew. These children should have been in school and growing up in a kinder, peaceful world. I found it difficult to accept. I remember wondering if anyone cared about these children. Part of me wanted to just walk away and ignore it, but I couldn't shake the image from my mind. I cared too much!

Climbing in Snow

Arabic lessons dragged on for months. "I really need to dig deep to keep the desire going," I wrote in an e-mail to our supporters. "It simply is a slog and one step at a time. It reminds me of climbing in snow . . .

"But," I continued, "friendship-building has been so encouraging. We both have good personal relationships. They help us with our Arabic, and we help them with their English. People here have a richness about them. They have been through so much, yet they are calm and thankful. Especially the believers, who have persevered and want to live a life controlled with God's love and kindness."

And so life went on. In many ways we began to feel more and more at home in Lebanon; in other ways the cultural strangeness and complexities of living in the Middle East continued to challenge us.

Cheryl Phenicie had started a prenatal clinic above the CMA church in Sidon. She and her husband, Daryl, were reaching out to the Palestinians at the refugee camp in Sidon called Ein el-Hilweh. Many of these people's parents had fled Palestine when Israel was being formed and they never returned. They lived illegally—with no real legitimate jobs or passports, or any amenities.

Cheryl wanted to help the pregnant women by providing a higher standard of health care. Every day the clinic doors were opened, women would pack the place, hoping to visit the doctor. Cheryl asked Bonnie to be a part of the ministry. Not only would it fulfill Bonnie's desire to serve the women of the region in a meaningful way, but it also would be an excellent opportunity to become more fluent in Arabic.

As Bonnie weighed her decision about working at the clinic, she admitted that she was scared. What if she didn't succeed? But after thinking and praying further, Bonnie decided to take the challenge. She would work at the clinic twice a week and eventually begin accompanying the doctor to the hospital when the babies were born.

I watched her life light up over the next year as she fell in love with her job and the women she was helping. After some months, Cheryl asked Bonnie if she would run the clinic while they were on furlough in the U.S. Bonnie agreed.

Bonnie wrestled with God in her journals—both questioning Him and yielding to Him, David-like. She longed to have a child, and her desire was sharpened by her work with Palestinian women at the prenatal clinic.

> *Dear Lord, I want to first of all thank You for helping me yesterday at the clinic. I was nervous because it was my first day, but I thank You because You gave me the courage and the strength to do it! God, I just want to surrender all my plans to You today. I want to give You the complete, utter control in my life. I want to lift You high above all else.*
> *—From Bonnie's journal: September 2001*

Who Will Love the Women?

Bonnie loved her work at the clinic. She had been restlessly wondering what God might have for her in Lebanon, and here was her opportunity.

She started her days at the clinic early, preparing for the women who would be coming that day. On one wall of the clinic was a bulletin board covered with snapshots of babies that had been born to the clinic's patients. Bonnie typically started her day filing the charts of the women who had been seen the previous day. The staff usually took a few minutes to pray together; then the secretary would write down the names of the women waiting to be seen that day and help Bonnie pull their charts. The clinic averaged about forty patients a day.

One by one, Bonnie weighed each patient and took their blood pressure, chatting with them cheerfully in Arabic while she made notations on their charts. Some of the women wore traditional Muslim dress, including headscarves; others came in maternity T-shirts. When Bonnie first began working at the clinic she spent most of her time visiting with the women in the waiting room, sharing her faith whenever an opportunity presented itself, sometimes giving out a Bible or a tract. As time went on, she began taking on more and more responsibility, working directly with the doctor. Sometimes she would share some of her clinic experiences in the prayer letter we sent out every few months:

> A girl came into the clinic. I was in charge that day when she came in to see the doctor. I went through all the normal questions with her: Where do you live? What is your blood type? However, when I asked her if she was pregnant she looked shocked. When I asked her what her husband's name

was, she just looked at me, startled, and said that she wasn't married.

It was the first time I had seen her. She said that she came from the Palestinian refugee camp. I asked her what she wanted to talk to the doctor about, and she said that she was having pain in her stomach. When her turn came, it turned out that the pain she was feeling was because she was six months pregnant. The truth came out eventually that she hadn't had relations with anyone, but her brother had raped her. Here she was, sitting in our clinic in shock. When we told her that she was pregnant she started to shake. Her whole body started convulsing from fear, shame, and anxiety. What would she do now? Who could she tell? Would her family find out the truth? You see, in Islam if a girl gets pregnant outside of wedlock and brings shame to the family, the family has the right to kill her. There was no way they would believe their daughter over their one and only son. The men in this culture are much more valued than women.

Her mom begged us to do an abortion but the doctor doesn't do abortions and told her again about how the baby was formed, that its heart was beating, that all its little bones and organs were already there. They left in denial and left us wondering if we would ever see her again. However, they did return the next week, and the doctor was able to convince her to try to stay in her house as much as possible, and he would do a C-section when she reached her eighth month. With a lot of prayer and pleading, we encouraged her to carry the baby and give it up for adoption. We told her about the love of God and His ability to heal and forgive all that had gone wrong. She finally decided after another month that she would give the baby up for adoption. This past Saturday she gave birth to a healthy seven-pound baby boy and gave him away so that he could have a better life.

Although these types of stories don't happen every day at the clinic, they are a lot more common than you might think. I have been serving at this prenatal clinic for the past nine months. We see mainly poor Palestinian women from the refugee camp nearby. Here in the Muslim world women are treated and seen as machines. They have only two functions: 1) to have children; 2) to make their husbands happy. They serve no other purpose. They are not cherished, supported, or loved. When they come into our clinic they receive something of the love of Jesus. We touch them and hug them and kiss them. We serve them coffee while they wait to see the doctor. We talk to them about their lives, about the good things and bad things, about their favorite foods. We let them talk about themselves. We try in any way possible to display to them the character of God, His grace and mercy and compassion. We also pray daily for God to help us create opportunities to explain to them about the Truth. . . .

I would really appreciate your prayers for me when I am in the clinic every Tuesday and Thursday. It is my burden to be able to talk to the women that come to the clinic about Jesus. This is the goal that I have for the clinic this year. I want many women to have an opportunity to hear about the love that Jesus has for them. Pray also that every piece of literature or Bible that leaves the clinic wouldn't return void. We are promised in the Bible that the word of God doesn't return void.

Also pray for protection for the women that come to the clinic. We have a lot of opposition to our work and really need

God's protection. Just recently I gave a woman a Bible while she was waiting for her turn. It turned out that when she went home her brother was drunk and beat her, stole money from her, and took the free clothes we had given to her for her baby. However, he didn't see the Bible, and she and her neighbor were fighting over who would read it.

While Bonnie worked, I spent time in a Bible Society bookshop engaging customers to sit down for Bible study. This "classroom" greatly increased my command of Arabic. We would have amazing conversations around a large table. All kinds of people came in—Catholics, Muslims, and evangelicals—and the conversation was always interesting.

Why Is Everyone Watching TV?

It was a warm, bright, hazy day in September and Bonnie had left for work at the clinic. That afternoon I was browsing in the Bible Society bookshop and I must have left about 3 p.m., making my way through the spillover of people from the shops onto the uneven sidewalks. On the way home I passed a shop where Bonnie and I bought lamps and other electronic items. I often stopped in the shop just to say hi. People knew I was a Bible teacher and Bonnie was working in the clinic. But they loved the fact that we also enjoyed living with them!

I didn't stop in the shop that day, but instead I decided to walk past the little taxi office run by a kind little man named Muhammad who loved to sit and have coffee with us when time allowed. I always enjoyed talking to him. He would often stop me and ask, "How is your health; how is your job; how is the apartment; how is your wife; how is your family in England; how is Bonnie's family?"

But I noticed as I walked past the shops that most of the shop-keepers were glued to a flickering on their TV sets. I could see pictures on the screens of big clouds of smoke. Had a volcano blown its lid, I wondered? I knew there was one in the Philippines that was being carefully monitored at that time. I finally stopped and couldn't believe what I saw—the Twin Towers in New York City had been attacked by terrorists. Stunned, I ran over to the local Internet café. The room was packed—and people were loud, shouting, celebrating! How could this be? I spoke briefly to the man standing next to me. "Why is everyone so happy?" He looked at me with a blank stare and just shrugged his shoulders.

I gathered with others in the café around one of the televisions and we watched replays over and over again of the plane flying into the first tower. The excitement of the crowd turned my stomach. I ran over to the little Arabic bookshop next to our apartment. I was friends with the workers there and wanted to talk to them about what was going on. But they, too, were happy. One of the men I had become friends with laughed and said, "Gary, is this good or bad?" His mother answered for me: "Bad," she said. Still she didn't seem too convinced.

I couldn't take any more. I ran up the stairs to our apartment, where Bonnie was home from the clinic and watching the TV in tears. She had seen it almost from the beginning. By the time I joined her, the first tower—and its occupants—was already gone. Meanwhile, out on the streets of Sidon, convoys of cars paraded up and down the streets, honking. Off in Ein el-Hilweh, the Palestinian refugee camp, we could hear rapid gunfire. Later I heard people were handing out candy. All over town a party was in progress.

After hours of just sitting and staring at CNN, Bonnie and I looked at each other in sorrow. We decided to risk venturing out to

Cheryl and Daryl Phenicie's place. It was a quick drive along the main road, and we arrived without incident. We felt drawn to one another by the horror. We all realized anew the frailty of life.

Suddenly we felt incredibly alone. Those people we had reached out to, those to whom we had explained God's forgiveness, were celebrating a horrendous and murderous act. We had to search deep for answers. Was it possible to keep reaching out with love to people who were mocking the suffering in New York?

A close pastor friend sent us an e-mail and asked us to seriously consider returning to the United States. Bonnie and I talked about what staying might mean. What if we were called to die for our faith? Would we be willing?

We looked at Matthew 6:27: "Who of you by worrying can add a single hour to his life?" and then Psalm 139: 15-16: "My frame was not hidden from you when I was made in the secret place. When I was woven together in the depths of the earth, your eyes saw my unformed body. All the days ordained for me were written in your book before one of them came to be."

We realized that no man could add or take a day from our lives. We decided to stay, no matter what.

☩

A year after September 11, 2001, a local newspaper article painted a different picture from the one we saw that day. Quotes from government officials called on the Lebanese to "show solidarity with the victims who were martyred in the United States at the hands of murderers whose acts are not legitimized by any law or religion." Camille Menassa of the Islamic-Christian National

Dialogue Committee said that Americans and Muslims should ask why animosity exists between the two cultures. And Olivia Ayyoub, whose son, Jude Moussa, died on the 105th floor of the North Tower, said, "I think we must find a solution to end terrorism everywhere, but it will not compensate for our loss."

Some months after the attacks, I wrote to our supporters:

> We have just come through a few crazy months. There were points when we really questioned our safety and other times we wondered if we could continue in Sidon. Now we have had Thanksgiving with friends and are preparing for Christmas. People here seem to care very little anymore about [the war in] Afghanistan. We had people burning American and British flags. The Sidon Mufti had everyone walk over an American flag as they entered into a mosque. We have had a bomb thrown at a church. Recently there have been two or three skirmishes at the Palestinian camp in Sidon. . . . "

We attended a retreat together with other Christian workers in Lebanon in May 2002 and were shocked when we learned that much of the retreat would be spent focusing on such issues as risk assessment, contingency planning, and evacuation training. There was a plan for surviving arrest and detention, and there was a plan for dealing with a "hostage event." If that happened, leaders urged the team, "Don't surrender your dignity, honor, or self-respect . . . don't feel you are forsaking God because you are dealing with emotional stress." We were all living in a new situation and didn't know what we might have to face in the coming months.

But despite our fears and the way our world seemed to be shifting beneath us, we knew more than anything else that we wanted to stay.

9

LIFE IS HARD, BUT GOD IS GOOD

*I feel I am on a journey of faith. What . . . do I do when
I've made my request to God, and the answer still has
not come? I need to keep on believing God's Word. I need
to hold on to God's character. I need to treasure the fact
that God is good and that He loves me more than anything in this world. He has a plan for me. He sees my
broken heart and my tears are not in vain.*
                    —From Bonnie's journal: May 12, 2002

More than anything, Bonnie wanted a baby.

When 2002 dawned, she wrote in her journal:

*Happy New Year to me! What a year this has been. So many
things happened this year it's hard to believe that we could
fit it all in one year. I was just telling Gary yesterday that if
we had been in Portland it would seem that just another year
had gone by. However, here it's different. This has been one
of the most memorable years of my life. I've loved it.*

*Even the really tough times have been such a blessing to me—
looking back I think one of the hardest times was trying to
deal with the September 11 attacks here in Saida [Sidon]. It
was eerie. We didn't know what people were thinking. We
didn't know how they would react. But now it seems we are
through that tense time, for the moment. And now the big-
gest thing I'm dealing with is trying to have a baby. I know
God knows when the right timing is. I know He has the situation under control. However, my yearning for a baby
increases month to month.*

We both were ready for a baby. And although we were trying to
conceive, God had not answered our prayers yet. It was painful
for Bonnie to watch others close to us being blessed with babies
when we were struggling. One of Bonnie's closest friends became
pregnant. Bonnie was the first one to know that she was pregnant.
Her friend had been nervous to tell her because she knew Bonnie
was longing so much for a baby. But when she did share the
news, Bonnie cried out with joy and laughter. The expectant
mother was relieved and grateful for Bonnie's willingness to set
aside her own desires and share in the happiness of her friend. It
wasn't until she got home that Bonnie cried quietly, as she prayed
for a baby of her own.

Bonnie stood by her friend every step of the way, including
the delivery which lasted for hours. We have a photo of Bonnie
holding the baby in her arms when he was just half an hour old.

Your Will, Not My Own

One day in the summer of 2002 Bonnie came bursting into the
apartment. Her face was radiant and her eyes were sparkling. New

Bonnie Witherall

Killed by a terrorist gunman on November 21, 2002,
while serving Jesus Christ and the Palestinian people at
a clinic in Sidon, Lebanon

Bonnie and I celebrate our engagement: December 14, 1996.

Bonnie is the picture of loveliness on April 19, 1997.

I enjoy showing off the English countryside to my Bonnie.

A spontaneous moment in England, only months before Bonnie was killed.

Dining with a view: Bonnie on the balcony
of our Sidon apartment

Our apartment building

A scenic view of Sidon. The Palestinian refugee camp where we served is in the foreground.

The street in Sidon where our apartment was located

Bonnie with the clinic doctor and Cheryl Phenicie, founder and director of the clinic

A photo gallery of babies whose mothers came to the clinic. Bonnie assisted in many of the deliveries.

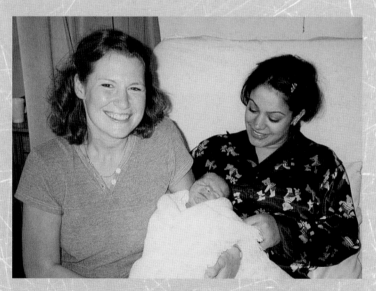

Bonnie holding a precious newborn beside a proud mother

"ورأيت عروشاً فجلسوا عليها وأُعطوا حكماً
ورأيت نفوس الذين قُتلوا من أجل شهادة يسوع ومن أجل كلمة الله...
فعاشوا وملكوا مع المسيح ألف سنة...
مبارك ومقدس من له نصيب في القيامة الأولى...*
(رؤيا ٢٠: ٤ و ٦)

كنيسة الاتحاد المسيحي الانجيلية الوطنية تدعوكم لمشاركتها في وداع المرسلة

بوني بينير ويذرول
Bonnie Penner Whitherall

التي قدمت حياتها على مذبح المحبة والخدمة في مستوصف صيدا المجاني
التابع لكنيسة الاتحاد المسيحي الانجيلية الوطنية

وذلك في مبنى كنيسة الاتحاد المسيحي الانجيلية الوطنية في صيدا – حي الدكرمان
تمام الساعة الثالثة من بعد ظهر يوم الأحد الواقع فيه ٢٤ تشرين الثاني ٢٠٠٢

The program for Bonnie's memorial service in Sidon, Lebanon, on November 24, 2002. Several hundred people attended.

Pastor Redwon, representing the Lebanese evangelical church, accompanied me to the United States for Bonnie's memorial service. Pastor Redwon died suddenly from a viral infection only months after this photo was taken.

I have had many amazing opportunities to share my story. One was a radio interview with fellow Moody Bible Institute grad, George Verwer, founder of Operation Mobilization.

I continue to serve God aboard missionary ships like the MV *Logos II*, challenging people to live in total abandon to God.

Only weeks after Bonnie's death, I spoke to students at Moody Bible Institute. Matt Edwards, who was my best man, sang the song "Surrender."

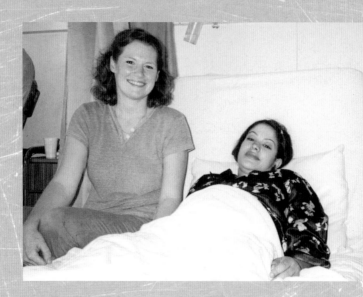

A happier time for Bonnie at the Sidon clinic

In March 2003, I visited the site where Bonnie was killed.

life was growing inside her! She was so excited she could hardly contain it. Finally! We hugged each other tightly; it was wonderful to see her joy and anticipation for the new life God had given us.

Over the next few months, our life seemed to center on this yet-to-be-born child of ours. Bonnie began buying baby clothing and we started making all the preparations new parents go through before their child arrives. As Bonnie helped other mothers-to-be prepare for their new babies, she now was able to compare notes about morning sickness, body changes, and dreams for the future.

The summer months were intense with joys and sorrows. While Bonnie was focused on working with the women at the clinic, I was involved with several opportunities for ministry. I joined two other fellow believers for a walking tour along the coast of Lebanon. We walked just over twenty miles a day for seven days. Along the way we distributed literature and shared the gospel. We prayed over every town and village as we traveled. Although the heat was brutal, the effort was rewarding. We finally came to the southern Lebanese border, which is secured by UN peacekeepers. At the border, we could see the land of Israel. I spent a couple of hours with the border guards, telling them about our ministry and sharing my story. They shared theirs as well. Many of the border guards were Fiji soldiers who were also believers and had seen a lot of suffering in southern Lebanon.

When we returned home, I looked for other opportunities to interact with the people in order to share God's love. I tried out and made a local soccer team. We traveled all over Lebanon playing soccer against other national teams. One of our games was in a Druze village in the mountains. The Druze (an offshoot of Islam) are some of the most unreached people in the area. After the game we gathered by the field and conducted an open-air meeting, which was practically unheard of in those parts. After every game we gave out Bibles and the *Jesus* film on video. We learned that sports ministries in the Middle East are very successful because they reach a part of the community that might not otherwise hear.

Back in Sidon, the doctor at the clinic checked our baby's heartbeat. "The heartbeat is very weak," he said gently to Bonnie. "The baby will probably not survive."

I was in the mountains when I received a call from a friend that I should return home to Bonnie in Sidon because something was wrong.

It was late in the evening as I drove down the mountain overlooking the bright lights of Beirut. I was worried about Bonnie. When I arrived home, she told me she had miscarried. She was devastated and as I held her in my arms, she burst into tears. I didn't know what to do or say. Bonnie had been so happy, so hopeful about starting our family. The day after our child died, I held Bonnie's hand while she lay on a hospital gurney, preparing to undergo a D & C.

I had no idea how much suffering women go through when they lose a baby. I could not console her; she was simply devastated.

Bonnie's miscarriage happened two days before we were scheduled to travel to England for a vacation. That evening we had to make a difficult decision. Should we still go to England as planned or should we stay? We finally decided that getting away might be the best thing for us, so the next day we flew out as planned. Bonnie grieved most of the fortnight, but my sister, Caroline, and her husband, Dean, lent us their house in Brighton while they were on vacation, which gave us needed rest and quiet. On August 16, 2002, Bonnie wrote in her prayer journal:

> *God, I know that You love me and I know that everything that happens in our lives is for our good. God, You alone know how much I wanted this baby. Thank You Lord that Your ways are perfect and that You love and care for me so much. God, I want to trust You again for another child. God, I want Your will to be accomplished in my life, not my own. It still hurts, God, not to have this baby, but I know it was the best for Gary and me. I want to thank You for Your mercy and kindness. Even though at the time I don't recognize it as Your mercy, I know You love us and the last thing You want to do is hurt us. God, help me to trust You. Help me to draw close to You during this time.*

> *God, I also want to thank You for all the good things You've provided for us this year. Your provision has been great, Lord. You've always been faithful to us.*

When our vacation was over, Bonnie prepared to return alone to Lebanon. I was flying to Canada to attend a friend's wedding. Bonnie had also been invited, but she really wanted to return to her work at the clinic. I had already left for Canada so my Dad drove her to the airport. As he said good-bye, he asked her,

"Are you afraid?"

"I'm not afraid at all," Bonnie said. "I'm going home."

When Bonnie returned home to Sidon, she e-mailed our friends to let them know what had been going on in our lives, and how God was helping us through it all:

Dear Friends,

Greetings from Lebanon! I am writing another "generic" e-mail to people because I want to explain to everyone who has been praying for us what God has been doing in my life over the last two weeks. I'm sorry that I couldn't write more personally but this is a lot easier. I hope you understand.

First of all, I want to thank all of you who have faithfully prayed for Gary and me during this really tough time that we have been going through (in regards to the miscarriage). We had a great time in England, and it was very clear that God had prearranged this time. He knew what was going to happen from the beginning, and we are so grateful that we had made a decision to go to England a while back. God is sovereign! The first week was really tough for me. I guess I just had so many questions for God and felt almost betrayed by Him. Of course this wasn't the case but that's how I felt in my heart. We were able to spend the first week in England by ourselves. Caroline, Gary's sister, and her husband let us house-sit for a week while they were on vacation. This was so good for us. Good for us to be alone and good for us to heal.

It's strange—during the second week and toward the end of my time in England I really felt the "heaviness" of the miscarriage and all the sadness and depression lift from me. Almost like God touched me and healed my heart. As I traveled back to Lebanon on the plane I experienced so much joy. I felt God's presence with me in a very real and tangible way. I was at the airport in London, sitting and drinking coffee, and God's presence was so real and so obvious that I just got out my journal right there and started talking to Him. When we flew into Beirut I started to cry. I really feel this is my home now and I felt for all the people here who are so lost and far from God.

Beyond any doubt I know that God loves me and what happened to me is not His fault. I have renewed faith in Him and, no matter what happens, know that He is good and I know and feel His undying and steadfast love for me! Thank you to all of you who really prayed for Gary and me. God has answered your prayers, and I wanted to share with you the joy that He has given me in the last few days! I know that the grieving is not over, and I have by no means forgotten about our little baby, but I know he/she is in heaven with Jesus and that is the best place for him/her.

God bless you all. Your support has been such a blessing and encouragement to us. We love you.

I returned from Canada and life for Bonnie and me fell into a familiar pattern. While our studies in Arabic continued to be challenging, we were getting better at it and thus better able to build relationships.

Bonnie and I learned that to survive in the Islamic world we needed to develop mental toughness. It wasn't the sort of toughness that could be taught in a classroom. It was about being prepared to be a living sacrifice daily. We knew it was our calling to love everyone all the time. Sometimes for Bonnie, the clinic was especially challenging:

Many times women come into the clinic with a "give-me" attitude. Actually, what's surprising is they come out and say it. There seems to be no shame. In America, or the West for that matter, we would never respond to someone giving us something for free by saying, "Is that all?" They are always complaining and hassling me, and it is to those conditions that Christ has called me. Sometimes I wonder if I'm really doing any good here at all. I feel discouraged because . . . our ministry at the clinic is more the action of Christ's love than the words. However, Jesus says to us that when we give a cup of cold water to "the least of these" we do it unto Him. Every time someone at the clinic asks me for a cup of water I give it to them, knowing I'm giving it to someone Jesus loves and cares for.

—From Bonnie's journal: November 9, 2002

On Monday, November 18, Bonnie and I spent the evening with Graham and Linda, our OM team leaders, and their family. Little did we know it would be Bonnie's last Monday alive. On the drive back home, we talked about what a nice time we had had. Then our conversation turned to our relationship and the vows we had taken when we had married. I thanked Bonnie for putting up with all of my shortcomings and for her love and commitment to me. I thank God now for the wonderful gift He gave me in allowing me to express my gratitude to my beautiful wife that night.

On Wednesday, Bonnie shared her testimony for the first time in Arabic with a local women's group at the Alliance Church. Most of these women were friends with Bonnie and not believers. That afternoon she had helped Dr. Edmond at the clinic with the patients from his own practice before leading our small prayer group for the workers in southern Lebanon. Every Wednesday night we got together to pray for each other and catch up on all that was going on in our lives. That night, Bonnie led the Bible study. She shone, and I sat back, proud of her as she taught from Hebrews 10.

Around 10 p.m. our guests left, and I said good night. As was her routine, Bonnie went to the computer to check her e-mail and see who was on MSN Messenger. That night Cheryl was online. Over the past year, Bonnie and Cheryl had grown very close, sharing a common enthusiasm for the ministry at the clinic. They began chatting on the Internet and became so excited talking about future plans and all the new things they were going to do in the clinic that Cheryl finally told Bonnie that she would have to call her to finish the conversation. They talked for over an hour that night.

When Bonnie came to bed, she was still excited about all that she knew God was going to do at the clinic. We said good night and fell asleep. We never spoke again.

In the morning she rose at about seven, probably smiling, and left quietly for the work she loved, taking care not to disturb me on my day off.

Then came that dreadful shrieking cry on the answering machine.

10

LAYING IT ALL DOWN

Lord, I want to commit myself to You once again.
Thank You for loving me unconditionally. Thank You
for sending Your Son Jesus into the world to forgive
us and to give us hope. Thank You for this beautiful
morning, Lord. Thank You for meeting all of our needs.
Thank You for Gary. . . .

—From Bonnie's journal

I stood in the center of the room where the soldiers had pushed me, water spilled at my feet, the white plastic cup still rolling along the edge of the floor.

"What's happening?" I yelled again.

Alison, part of the clinic team, spoke up. "Bonnie is dead," she said, barely able to get the words out. "She's been killed."

Suddenly I was wrenched into a place I could never have imagined. An hour earlier, I had been happy to sleep in, peaceful and thankful for all that God had given me—us—in life. Our life. Now I was forced to fall and fall and fall into the abyss of grief. I was not ready for this. I was not given time to prepare for the loss of the one person who lit up my world. *Boom*, there I was, forced into a world of agony.

Broken by the news hitting me, I fell to the floor. I did not know I could cry so hard or feel so alone. I am a happy, content person by nature. I love life and all the great challenges waiting out there. Now I, like Bonnie, lay on the floor.

I thought maybe the gunman was waiting for me. Waiting to rush in and shoot me dead too. I buried my face in the floor and wondered when I would get it. My body began to shake, and I could feel myself falling into shock, something I recognized from when I had been in the motorbike accident in England years before. I felt all alone, exposed. Our beautiful world, our safe love, breakfast on the balcony with Bonnie's German crepes and good coffee, talking about life—gone. Bonnie, my best friend, this wonderfully gentle person who loved the women in the clinic with laughter and tears—gone. I could still picture Bonnie crying out on Navy Pier in Chicago: "I'm getting married!" Our beautiful journey we had so loved to share had come to an end.

As I tried to process all that was happening, I felt the Lord say to me, *There has been a seed planted in your heart. It is a seed that will grow from anger to hatred—or from forgiveness to love. It is a choice you need to make now.*

You're right, Lord, I told Him. Either way it would be a decision people would understand. But how could I forgive this? It was impossible.

It felt as if the Lord was taking me to the cross, and it was as if I was looking through His eyes as He hung on the cross. His blood, falling with tears, as He cried out in His suffering, "Father, forgive them, they do not know what they are doing." I knew I was the one who had helped Him to that cross. All the garbage of my life, my failings and sin. It was as if I was one of those soldiers mocking Him. I was one He had forgiven of so much sin.

I convulsed with everything in me as I said aloud, "Lord, I forgive them." It was the message I had been preaching everywhere during our time in Lebanon. It was a message I believed—I knew I had been forgiven of all the garbage in my life. And here and now, with God's help, I realized that I *could* show a forgiveness that was way beyond me. In forgiving whoever had killed Bonnie, I gave Jesus the right to judge. This was the greatest test of my life. I would never be able to give more, or show greater forgiveness. I had to live in faith that God was in control, that Bonnie was with Jesus in heaven. I chose to believe the Bible, to believe that God knew, and now I needed to trust Him.

A familiar song came into my head. I felt I was being called to lay down everything for Him in surrender.

> I'm giving You my heart and all that is within
> I lay it all down for the sake of You, my King
> I'm giving You my dreams, I'm laying down my rights
> I'm giving up my pride for the promise of new life
> And I surrender all to You, all to You
> I'm singing You this song, I'm waiting at the cross
> And all the world holds dear, I count it all as loss
> For the sake of knowing You, the glory of Your name
> To know the lasting joy, even sharing in Your pain
> And I surrender, all to You.
> Used with permission of Vineyard Songs (UK/Eire).

Making the Headlines

The room was filling with soldiers and police, and they all wanted to talk to me. Many of them were smoking, some were laughing; it all seemed so surreal. I couldn't believe the situation. Although I still had not been allowed to see Bonnie, many of the soldiers walked freely in and out of the clinic. There seemed to be little control over who was there or what was being done. I told someone who seemed to be in authority to clear the room, and slowly the large group shuffled out.

As soon as the room cleared, someone came in and told me Bonnie's body had been taken but I had no idea where. Panicked, I stood up and walked to the door, where a cameraman was focusing in on me, probably for a close-up of my reaction. I put my hand up, went back into the room, and shut the door. But enough footage had been shot for CNN to use. In the hours that followed, my parents in England were shocked when they sat down to watch the news and saw their son on television.

People were starting to converge on the clinic. Representatives from the U.S. Embassy arrived and quickly secured the building. One of the staff members rushed up to me and looked into my eyes. I was completely broken and still fearful of being killed myself. He said, "We are here to protect you. Nothing will happen to you now." Two other staff people put a blanket around me and sat next to me to help as best they could. Then the British consul and a bodyguard with a Union Jack on his jacket arrived. I began to tell them a little bit of what I understood had happened, which was not a lot at that point. Soon after, others arrived: Graham arrived from his home in the mountains followed by other friends including our pastor and his wife from our church in Mieh Mieh. The media were swarming all over the place, they said.

Graham said we needed to call Bonnie's parents. It was important to do that quickly; I didn't want Al and Ann in Washington to get the news secondhand. I could not even imagine how they would take the early morning news. Over and over I played the scenario of that phone call in my mind. It had been my job to protect their daughter; her parents had entrusted her to me. How could I deliver such horrible news to them now? I was grateful when Graham offered to make the call.

"Who would do such a thing?" Al asked when he got the news. Who, indeed?

I called the Thurmans, friends from Portland, and asked if they would go over and be with the Penners. I thought they would be the ones who could help the most; the Thurmans had been like parents to us in Portland and had ministered in Sidon before the civil war. And in 1997, I had watched them mourn the loss of their younger son, Jonathan, who was killed in a car accident in California while he was at college. Pat had told me how one day he was walking across the room in his house and collapsed to his knees in grief.

I then had to think about my parents. I couldn't bear to think of just anyone calling them with the news, so I asked Graham to find the number for Keith, our old pastor from Crawley Community Church. He hurried over to my parents' home, and they watched me on CNN shortly after his arrival.

Sami Dagher, the director of the CMA church in Lebanon, arrived, overcome with sorrow. He was both a good friend of ours and pastor of the church below the clinic.

"I want to go into the clinic for a moment," I said. He went in with me. The floor was still covered in blood; in fact, there was blood all over the room. I could look at it only briefly, and yet the image is still burned into my mind. It all felt like a very bad dream. Only later would I learn that it was Pastor Sami who got on his knees and cleaned up the blood. I was humbled by his action and will never forget what he did for me that day.

The Government Takes Over

We were all very grateful for how professionally the U.S. embassy staff took care of the situation. I felt very safe, and when it came time to leave the building, they took great measures to ensure all of our safety. Sidon, of course, was my home, and until now I had never felt afraid to be there. I later learned that Bonnie was the first American to be killed in Lebanon in thirteen years. As I cracked open the blinds and looked down at the street where throngs of photographers, journalists, and those who were merely curious amassed, I was struck by how bizarre the whole scene was. The embassy people rearranged the vehicles, and one by one all of us—U.S. embassy staff, clinic workers, and myself—were motioned to the door by a man who wore an earpiece with a coiled wire leading to a lapel microphone. Now they were fully in charge. Two men, one on each side, led me down the stairs. One man had his hand behind my head and pushed it downward. Suddenly we moved very quickly. I felt like I was in a movie. I was pushed into a white Suburban, and then the doors locked.

What a strange feeling it was to be speeding up a road that either Bonnie or I had walked on nearly every day, a neighborhood where we knew many of the shop owners. Convulsed with weeping, I wished I could just go to sleep and pretend this wasn't happening.

The vehicles pulled away, sirens blaring, broadcasting an automated message in Arabic that warned people to step aside. We were off to the Sidon courthouse to meet the judge who would preside over this case. The motorcade moved very quickly, and inside the car I was being briefed by the embassy staff about what I should and should not say. None of us knew who had shot Bonnie or why she had been targeted.

When we arrived at the courthouse we first were led into a large office with some senior officials who gave us Arabic coffee and briefed us about what would take place next. We were shuttled off to the judge's chambers. By this point I was completely exhausted and emotionally drained, but my body would not allow me to sleep because of the adrenaline running through my system. As we were questioned, a court stenographer slowly typed out our conversation on an old typewriter. The judge, well dressed in a suit, began to unfold the story, asking multiple questions. At one point Bonnie's navy blue backpack—the same one she had carried in her Moody student days—was brought to him from the clinic, along with her purse, keys, cell phone, jewelry, and a few other things. It seemed I had been forced to go over and over the story countless times already throughout the day and now I had to tell what I knew again at great length.

It was four in the afternoon when the tedious interrogation finally concluded. Outside the courthouse, Graham sat waiting in the Range Rover with another Christian leader and close friend. He looked at me, burst into tears, and put his arms around me. My mind flashed back to the first time he and I had met. We had just arrived in Beirut and were shopping in a bookstore on Hamra Street, the main shopping drag. After introducing ourselves and talking a bit, I had asked him, "Do you have any advice for me about Lebanon?" He turned, looked me square in the eye and said, "I don't care what you do, just as long as you have fun. If you have fun, everything else will be okay." Then he turned back to his books and carried on with what he was doing.

That small piece of advice went a long way. Now here he was, standing in front of me, broken by the reality of what had happened. I was being evacuated from Sidon, along with all the other foreigners. We decided that I should go to my apartment to pick up anything that I might want, because this might be my last chance. At the same time, the other foreigners were also packing to leave for Beirut. I climbed into the Range Rover, and we drove down my road, past many of my friends in their stores, to my apartment block. I knew that by this time, most of them would have heard the news. We rushed up the stairs, and in a new, strange way, I opened my front door. It was glossy white with a wood frame. I had just painted the stairwell walls, and it looked really good.

I opened the door for what would be the last time and the late-afternoon sun was streaming through the room. God had given us such a beautiful place to live—a true refuge. I had five minutes to pack things I really wanted. In our bedroom, the bed was unmade, and Bonnie's clothes still lay on the floor. She had this funny habit of getting dressed, changing her mind, throwing the clothes on the floor, and wearing something else. I could still smell her perfume on the pillows, on the bedding we had brought from America. I sat on the edge of the bed and looked out on the blue Mediterranean one more time. The view looked the same as it had the first day we had arrived in Sidon almost two years earlier, alive with joy and expectation.

I quickly gathered a few of my clothes, some books, my computer, and a few other personal possessions. I dumped everything into our suitcases. I paused to look at the office desk and Arabic couch I had made, the maps on the wall, and all of our Arabic language study papers lying around. This place that had been so warm and vibrant now had become part of a smashed dream.

Hang Your Sword on the Wall

We drove to Graham and Linda's house in the mountains above Beirut. Linda offered me food but I refused, thinking, *I never want to eat again.* "You have a lot to face," she said. "You need to keep your strength up." There in the mountains I was too cold to drink water, and because I was already shaking I didn't want coffee or tea. So she prepared warmed orange juice for me. At any other time I would have thought, *This is disgusting,* but on this day it was perfect.

Phone calls began flooding in—family members, church leaders, people I had never heard of before. The calls kept coming, and I kept taking them, until two in the morning. Every time I took a call it seemed my whole body just shook, and I cried loudly. Finally Graham encouraged me to unplug the phone. My face was sore and swollen from weeping. It felt like sandpaper, and my tears burned my skin. Graham's son had let me stay in his room, and there I was, lying in his bed alone. The pain and places where my mind was taking me were really awful, but in the midst of it all, I felt as if the Lord physically had His arms around me. It is a phenomenon I can't explain. It was as if someone was hugging me from behind. I felt the sensation for many months afterward. On this night I lay in the strange bed, sleepless, broken, asking the Lord for strength.

During the night there was a moment when I suddenly felt I was in the presence of God. It was like I was in a bright room, and I sensed Him speaking to me. I had always seen myself as a soldier of the Cross, with the power of the gospel as my sword. But on this night, it was as if the Lord said to me, "Pull out your sword and hang it on the wall." I saw myself pulling the sword out of its scabbard on my hip and hanging it vertically on the wall. The sword looked well worn, dinged and nicked from the battles I had waged throughout my years of ministry and travel. Somehow it also reflected my successes and failures. Then I felt the Lord say to me,

"Step back and look at your life. It's been good." I remember thinking, *Yes, it's been an amazing experience.*

And the Lord said, "Leave your sword on the wall. That's done. I have a new sword for you." The next thing I saw was His brilliant arm, handing me a sword that dazzled with light. "Put it in your scabbard," He said. With that, the whole vision ended.

I don't know if I even slept that night. I felt so close to the Lord; I knew that He understood my anguish.

In a moment when everything in my life had been stripped away, in a moment when I might have fallen into an abyss of despair, I found myself standing on a rock—safe, immovable. Some years before I had visited Tintagel, a small Cornish village with a ruin of a castle. Legend has it that this was the castle of King Arthur and his Knights of the Round Table. The castle sits high above the Atlantic atop granite crags. I watched as the huge swells of the North Atlantic pounded the English coastline—but the ancient rock stood defiant.

> Rock of ages, cleft for me, let me hide thyself in thee.

That, I believe, is what it means to have Christ in your life. It's only a matter of time until each of us is tested by some challenge that we cannot meet with our own strength. Who will help us? Where does our hope come from? The thought took me straight to Psalm 121:

> I lift up my eyes to the hills—where does my help come from?
> My help comes from the LORD, the Maker of heaven and earth.
> He will not let your foot slip—he who watches over you will not
>   slumber;
> Indeed, he who watches over Israel will neither slumber nor sleep.

The LORD watches over you—the LORD is your shade at your right
hand;
The sun will not harm you by day, nor the moon by night.
The LORD will keep you from all harm—he will watch over your life;
the LORD will watch over your coming and going both now and
forevermore.

Suddenly I had this thought:

I remembered the day that my beautiful bride walked up the
aisle to marry me, how she had shone in her stunning white
dress. Now in white she walked from this dark world into the
presence of Christ. My wife, a bride, a martyr, beginning her new
life in paradise.

There was no turning back and I couldn't undo what had happened. Even if I didn't fully understand it, I trusted the Lord.

11

A PRINCESS
OF THE KINGDOM

*My life is simply sustained with a violent awe in the arms of
Jesus, holding me as if I can feel them.*
                    —*From Gary's journal: December 2002*

For six years almost everything I did, I had done with my best
friend. From this point on I would be doing everything alone.
Already it felt strange.

Friday, the day after Bonnie's death, newspapers everywhere
were covering the story. Media attention, I discovered, is an interesting animal. It seems to pounce on someone in crisis. There we
were living our life one day in obscurity, then suddenly Bonnie's
gone and I was besieged by press from around the world trying
either to get a taped interview or to write a story about the events
using what little information they could piece together.

Overall, I was encouraged by the positive message they communicated. A reporter from *The Times* of London called requesting an
interview. I know how the press can put a spin on their coverage

and said to him, "You are living in a politically correct world. And if you are man enough to write what I say, I will give you the interview." I was in no mood to entertain journalists. But sure enough, the next day on the front page of *The Times*, my words were printed just as I said them. And the story went around the world. I was pleased with how they portrayed my wife and her life. But I was still alone.

Yesterday You Became One of Us

On Friday I also met with many of the Christian leaders in Lebanon at Sami Dagher's home. The room was thick with an air of shock and grief; it was difficult for me to contain the tears that threatened to spill over at any time. We agreed that the CMA church below the clinic was the appropriate place for a memorial service on Sunday evening. My pastor from the Mieh Mieh church outside Sidon looked me in the eye and said, "You foreigners will always be looking from the outside in. It will always be impossible for you to understand the pain and cost to us going through the civil war. But yesterday you became one of us." I was amazed by his words; it was a kind thing to say. In my spirit I knew that for the rest of my life I would be connected with the church in Sidon.

On Saturday Graham and I went to Beirut so that I could buy a suit for the service. I picked out a plain black suit. The shop manager urged me to try on something a little flashier. I said no. Black shoes, black tie, black socks. I went into the fitting room and put the suit on. As I looked in the mirror, I felt like collapsing. I had lost Bonnie. I hadn't worn a suit for years, most recently at our wedding. Now I had to act and dress a certain way, be someone I wasn't. What more could be taken away?

On Sunday morning, November 24, I met with the American ambassador Vincent Battle in Beirut. He was visibly moved by the whole story. We sat and spoke at length about the situation and he offered any support he could give.

I knew he had a tough job ahead. There were all kinds of people who could have been involved with this murder. With anti-American feeling pretty high in Lebanon it would be a tough challenge to find who was behind the attack. Some said it was because the clinic and church were so popular in the city, while others said the motives were to attack the United States.

Sunday afternoon we drove down to Sidon, where hundreds of people packed the little church and hundreds more waited out-side. I was escorted into a room full of top Christian and political leaders, as well as the sister of Prime Minister Ratik Hariri. They were all there in person to tell me—and the public—that this trag-edy was unacceptable, that the Lebanese government was angered by this attack. Several of the leaders were talking to one another, and as they talked, it was clear that tensions were rising when the talk focused on attacks against Christians. Some even began to argue. I sat there, listening to them bicker as I fought back the tears. It felt surreal. Several TV cameras were trying to force their way into the room. My pastor stood behind me and translated all that was being said. I asked if I could say something, and the room became quiet.

"I remember as a child back in England, watching the continu-ous news coverage of the Lebanese war. I still have the visual images in my mind of newsreels showing rockets being fired," I said. "People always talk about political solutions. But even if there is political resolution, there is still anger in the heart. The problems of Lebanon are not going to be solved by political arguing. I believe the message of forgiveness is a message that Lebanon needs."

We all walked into the church sanctuary and the memorial service began. Graham stood and addressed the crowd. He shared stories from Bonnie's past, including tales I had told him about our days at Moody. "Gary told me today that from the first time he and Bonnie sat down and talked, there was almost something sacred about their friendship," Graham said. "[He] thought she was like a princess of the Kingdom of God."

He was right. Bonnie had been a princess in God's kingdom. I had known it even then. Graham mentioned how hard Bonnie had worked to show her love to me in our marriage and how much she cherished all the relationships in her life.

"They were rich and deep relationships, as many of us here know," he said. "They were full of love—God's love. One of her favorite things to talk about was her relationship with the women in the clinic. Her eyes would light up as she recounted the many experiences and friends that she had there. She found great satisfaction in serving others in the name of Jesus. She felt that showing love practically was something that she should and could do."

Graham remembered one day when a friend had asked Bonnie, "What would you like to have written on your tombstone?" Bonnie's reply? "Have them write, 'She lived life to the full.'"

In the book of Revelation we read that there is a special place under the altar of God reserved for those who have given their lives for the sake and the service of the Lord Jesus. I knew this was the place where I would one day see Bonnie again. I prayed that God would help me to stand strong until that day. Bonnie had run the race before us. She was faithful to the end, serving Him even when He called her home.

Everything I Am

At the back of the church the press was packed in with cameras and recorders. I stood to speak to the crowd:

> To the President of Lebanon, the Prime Minister, and the Speaker of the House,
>
> I'd like to say, I love Lebanon; I love her people and my hometown, Sidon. I'd like to start by thanking the people from Lebanon and from around the world for their e-mails, phone calls, and prayers.
>
> Some people may think the death of my wife was a waste. Bonnie and I came to Lebanon understanding only a small part of the pain this country has gone through, but we believed that coming with a message of Jesus which gives hope, love, and forgiveness would never be a waste. This is a message for hurting people in a suffering generation. And this message is worth laying down our lives for.
>
> I want to say "thank you" to the people of Sidon and southern Lebanon for allowing us to make this our home. We felt loved and part of the community. I want to let whoever did this crime know that I forgive them. It's a forgiveness that costs me everything that I am, but I can forgive because I know God, through Jesus' blood, has forgiven me. The blood of Jesus was poured out for the sins of the world, and when Bonnie's [blood] poured across the clinic [floor] on Thursday morning, she showed the same love for the women of Sidon.

I stood outside at the end of the service and shook everybody's hand as they left the church. I was overwhelmed by the response of many of the believers from around Lebanon. Many of our Muslim friends were also there. While I was hugging and talking to people, a sea of media swarmed the area, recording the scene. Afterward I held a news conference, answering reporters' questions one by one. A journalist from a French newspaper in Lebanon asked again and again about my reaction toward whoever had cut Bonnie's life short. The journalist seemed to have a difficult time comprehending the fact that I was willing to forgive the person or persons responsible. In her world, in the Middle East, when something like this happens the normal response is anger and a thirst for revenge.

But I didn't want to set myself up as some kind of model Christian. I didn't have the strength to be any more than what I am. It's quite simple: Everything that I am tells me that Christ is in control of my life. He knew what He was doing when He allowed Bonnie to be taken.

When we got back into Pastor Sami Dagher's car, his cell phone began to ring. It was Franklin Graham. He offered words of encouragement, saying that he believed my testimony was going to have a powerful impact. He believed God was going to do great things through Bonnie's death. As we talked, I felt as if he were speaking directly to my future.

This had been one of the most difficult days I had ever experienced, but through it all, I sensed Christ Himself standing right beside me.

That evening many of my friends and I went out for a meal with Pastor Sami. As we gathered over wonderful Lebanese food, I looked at Sami and sensed the personal responsibility he felt for Bonnie, since he oversaw the clinic. I realized then that our hearts would always be locked together, because it was he who cleaned up Bonnie's blood from the clinic floor. Sami Dagher was broken. He had spent his life ministering to his war-torn nation, sharing the gospel with a people who so desperately need it. I looked at him and my heart was overwhelmed with love for him.

On Tuesday I met with another group of people in a room near Beirut, friends who had been close to Bonnie and me. I told the story of her death again, and then we spent time in prayer and worship. I wondered if this was how the early church had felt, meeting secretly during a time of persecution.

Some friends had given me Michael W. Smith's *Worship* CD the previous summer, and Bonnie had regularly played it during her walks along the beach in Sidon. I listened to it often in the days following her death. As the music flooded my soul, I found myself thinking again and again of Bonnie, of her love for the Lord, and of her passion for the people of Lebanon. One of the songs seemed to be especially meaningful to me now. In the middle of "Let It Rain: Open the Floodgates of Heaven, Let It Rain," someone cries out Psalm 97:1-6:

> The LORD reigns, let the earth be glad;
> Let the distant shores rejoice.
> Clouds and thick darkness surround him;
> Righteousness and justice are the foundation of his throne.
> Fire goes before him and consumes his foes on every side.
> His lightning lights up the world;
> The earth sees and trembles.
> The mountains melt like wax before the LORD,
> Before the LORD of all the earth.
> The heavens proclaim his righteousness,
> And all the peoples see his glory.

As I prayerfully meditated on the words of Scripture in song, I felt that the Lord would use Bonnie's death as one of the ways to answer this prayer. Many people would see God's glory through this tragedy. Certainly in this week alone, many newspapers had already clearly communicated the message of the forgiveness that is found in Christ. From that moment I believed God was going to do great things through an act that had been meant for great harm.

12

A LONG JOURNEY

Nothing remains, and yet I have everything. I lost my wife, my ministry, my beautiful apartment overlooking the Mediterranean, my friends there, my Arabic classes, and three classes a week studying Islam. The little Honda we drove on the bumpy roads through the crazy traffic. The warmth of Bonnie lying quietly asleep next to me. I was robbed but have been found today steadfast, strong as a piece of steel yet completely broken. Lord, sustain me.

—From Gary's journal: December 11, 2002

The airport in Beirut boasts a new, sterile-white terminal. A week after grieving on the clinic floor stained by my wife's blood, I was in the Beirut airport, on my way to the United States via Amsterdam. It was time to take Bonnie home. It had been a week of endless phone calls, official interrogations, and media interviews. Now the first secretary of the U.S. Embassy in Beirut met my colleagues and me and helped us get through security quickly. On the KLM flight I had hours to sit, so I listened to a worship CD and thought about all that had happened, including the fact that my wife's body was below me in a box.

As I walked off the Jetway in Amsterdam, a man came up to me with a cell phone. He asked my name and gave me the phone, saying it was the FBI calling. I felt as if I was suddenly part of a strange new world. How did he know who I was? The FBI agent said they wanted to do an autopsy on Bonnie's body once we arrived in the United States. It was another word that had to sink in: *autopsy*. My wife's autopsy.

Over the past week I had dealt with people I would never have wanted to meet. The coroner in Sidon, sweaty, with wispy gray hair, looking at me with tears in his eyes, shaking his head in silent disbelief over the terrible thing that had taken place in his city. His grief typified so many people in Lebanon.

The plane left Amsterdam in the morning light. I wept almost continuously, keenly aware that the seat next to me was empty. Before I met Bonnie I felt as if I were always flying away from people I loved. But after I met Bonnie I had rejoiced in traveling with my best friend. Now the flight, and the tears, went on and on and on.

We arrived in Seattle on Thanksgiving Day. The airport was almost deserted, quiet except for the noise of a football game blaring on the TV above the baggage claim carousels. I watched and thought of all the families across the country gathered around festive tables, all the men relaxing before the game. Bonnie loved cooking Thanksgiving dinner and had already sent out invitations to friends for the feast she had planned for us that year. I wondered if it was okay not to be thankful.

Lynden, Washington, is a little Dutch farming community where beautiful houses now surround golf courses. Beyond Lynden, miles and miles of farmhouses and steel silos sit under the shadow of the mountain ranges on the Canadian side, while Mount Baker dominates the horizon on the Washington side. Here Bonnie's dad, Al, had desperately tried to teach me to play golf; here he had beaten me in one-on-one games of basketball in the driveway.

When I reached the Penners' home, the door opened, and the three of us fell into one another's arms. We didn't talk about what happened. Not yet. Later I would tell the story, with anguish and in detail. Right now we simply held one another.

A Hole in the Ground

On the morning after Thanksgiving, with a dizzying sense of unreality, I donned my funeral suit so I could bury my wife.

Surprisingly, I had never been to a funeral. This was the first time I had ever sat by an empty hole in the ground. A large crowd of friends and family gathered for the service under the light-blue sky with Mount Baker in the background. The funeral director stood next to me chatting about caskets. Bill Perkins, the pastor who had counseled us, married us, and still felt like family to me, shared a message of hope. I wondered how he could stand up there talking. Al and Ann sat staring straight ahead in their chairs.

After the service, people drifted away. This was the moment I had dreaded for the last eight days, the moment the cemetery workers would come and lower the casket into the ground with a manual winch that works with gravity. I watched, not turning my eyes away, even though it felt as if I were seeing it in a dream. It occurred to me that Bonnie and I had died to ourselves a long time ago.

When I came back to Al and Ann's house, I rushed to the room I always shared with Bonnie when we visited and changed into my own clothes, tossing everything into the clear garment bag that came with the suit. I had an overwhelming sense of being violated, as if I had been wearing death itself. I tied the bag with its clothes into a ball. Some of my friends outside joined me and kicked it around the yard like a soccer ball. Kicking death around helped. I recommend it.

The Fellowship of the Fire

I felt a deep desire to renounce death in my life, to banish the thought of bullets ending beautiful Bonnie. I had to dispose of the death-clothes. I called my close friends to join me. We stopped at a local grocery store, picked up a load of firewood, and drove out to Birch Bay on the Washington coast. Bonnie, her parents, and I had gone for a long walk along the ocean there right before we left for Lebanon. It was a special place that held unforgettable memories.

It was freezing cold when we gathered on the beach. A deep fog had set in so we could not see more than fifty feet in front of us. We started a fire in a fire pit and pulled some benches around it. The raw weather seemed appropriate; tonight was a night to encourage each other. It was a night for some of my closest friends to grieve together with me. Slowly the blaze of the fire warmed the air immediately around us. My brother Jonathan had brought out a guitar and for the next hour we sang old songs from Bob Dylan to Paul Simon. We laughed and sang loudly in our grief. We talked about how strange it had been to deal with the press during such a personal, traumatic time. We all shared our memories of this amazing woman who had been my wife. We reminisced about earlier, more innocent times. And more.

I handed everything I had worn to Bonnie's funeral—the suit, shirt, tie, socks—to my friends. Each one said a few words and then threw the garments on the raging fire. I looked around at the guys.

My closest friends, most of them at least, were here. It was a moment I knew I would never forget. As the clothes turned to ashes, we renounced the sting of death. I knew Bonnie had passed from this weary world into a beautiful eternity.

As we watched the fire burn, our weary hearts found a moment of strength in the long process of dealing with what life had just thrown our way. Graham said, "This was men grieving as men." Together, with intensity. One of my friends turned and said, "This is the fellowship of the fire." As the night moved on, we began to pray and sing to the Lord. Suddenly, the mist lifted and we could see out over the water.

MAIL MESSAGE

Dear Friend,

Please forgive this impersonal e-mail. But I so want to connect with people these days that I risk sending you this note from the heart. It is December 23rd and I am in the air. I just left Frankfurt Airport. For a week I have been quiet and reflective with a friend and mentor, someone who has known me now over fifteen years.

If I could sit and have coffee with you right now, and we shared a few thoughts, perhaps this is what you would hear. I have been overwhelmed by the love, care, and concern people I have known for years have shown me in this time. It has of course been the greatest tragedy of my life and the loss of my beautiful wife is unparalleled to any kind of experience I can conceive. I loved her more than myself. Yet in these days I have such peace with God. I sense such strength that through my burning tears the Lord has remained faithful to me. One thing I consider as I sit here with our wedding rings now on my leather necklace [is that] I was God's man for Bonnie's life and I was the one chosen to love, respect, and serve her as she was to follow Christ's higher calling.

I hope you can smile with me over Bonnie's life and understand that today she is dancing with Jesus. I have often thought of the fact that I, too, was not killed. It would have been easier for me. The fact remains that I still have a role God wants me to play here.

Someone reminded me the other day that Bonnie is having her best Christmas ever. So with that, I wish you a Merry Christmas. One where Christ makes sense and His joy will be as present in your life as it is in mine.

I was amazed at the friends who came to stand by me during the greatest horror of my life. People came from many countries and across the United States. I was also struck by the outpouring of love and grief on the part of those I didn't even know. I received an influx of e-mails from across the globe, from India to Brazil. People wrote to let me know they were praying for me in Korea and Belarus. I was surprised to find our story in newspapers everywhere and I was grateful for the high percentage of positive coverage we received.

December 25, 2002

Christmas morning, sitting in Bill Perkins's front room after bacon, eggs, and crumpets. I can see Mt. Hood through the window with its fresh coating of snow above Timberline. Yesterday I went looking for a new snowboard. I didn't sleep well; it's strange waking up by myself. I don't like it. I miss Bonnie being excited, insisting she open a gift on Christmas Eve. I feel lost in this new world. It is comforting to be in Portland, visiting places we used to go together. It is just that I miss my bride.

—From Gary's journal

Questions

"Why? Why Lebanon? Why the Middle East? Why would you put yourselves at such risk?"

I heard these questions often. After Bonnie was killed, a little more than a year after jets flew into the Twin Towers and the world became aware of a new evil arising out of the Islamic world, people wanted to know if I regretted our decision to minister in Lebanon. The question deserves a thoughtful response. The simplest answer is this: Bonnie and I were two people who loved Jesus, longed to live for Him completely, and had a passion to share His love with a hurting world. We went where He sent us, dangerous or not. He did not call us to a place, He called us to Himself. We had known that we wanted to live fully and we both did. A thought keeps occurring to me as I reflect on these questions: "If it is not worth dying for, is it worth living for?"

13

THE ASTONISHMENT
OF HIS GRACE

*Dear Jesus, Today I read Your Word about loving our
enemies. God, we have so many enemies these days . . .
In Romans 12 You tell us not to repay anyone evil for
evil, but rather to be careful to do what is right in the
eyes of everybody. To live at peace with all men. Leave
room for God's wrath.*

—From Bonnie's journal

Then came the "now what."

Early in 2003 I settled in Atlanta, the U.S. headquarters of Operation Mobilization. Family and friends surrounded me with support
and compassion. As people began to hear of Bonnie's death, invitations for me to speak poured in. Gradually I began to sense
God's nudging me toward a new kind of ministry.

There was—and is—pain. Some images will never go away. I think
of the gunman. And I think of Bonnie's father, Al. Months after
Bonnie's death, we sat in his backyard on a cool evening. I looked
at the soft lines on Al's face, a face I had come to love. I wondered
if the gunman had thought of a loving father having to live the rest

of his life without his little girl. With each of our lives broken, Al and I talked. His face was gripped with sorrow as he looked at me and said, "If I had known Bonnie would be a martyr perhaps I might have done things differently. . . ." Then he caught himself. He couldn't have known.

I've returned to Lebanon several times since Bonnie was killed. In the autumn of 2004, everything looked pretty much the same, with one exception. Dark-green ivy is now beginning to curl around the locked gates outside the deserted CMA church and clinic, and the entrance is littered with garbage.

The building seems to reflect life in Lebanon, a nation with a proud and ancient history of Christianity dating back centuries before Islam invaded from the East. But now, because of fear, threats, and murder, the church has been forced to close. Now this little church that provided so much to the community when we lived there has ivy tangling the gates that once opened to all in need.

I was conscious of a sense of violation—and a vacant silence. My wife was murdered; life goes on. Nobody speaks up, nobody cries for justice. If anyone did want to speak out, he would do so at peril to his life. The interest has waned; the media have moved on to covering the war in Iraq. That's the big news now.

They still have not officially caught Bonnie's killer. In October 2004 in Lebanon a large Al-Qaeda cell group was captured. The leader, who some said was Bonnie's killer, died within a week in prison. But neither the FBI nor the Lebanese government has ever told me that they officially know who did it. I do not know if we will ever know. What is most important is that God *does* know and He will bring justice.

The following excerpts from my journal and various letters and poems thread together the "what now" and "what next."

I've Lived Thirty Years in Six Weeks

From an e-mail to friends and supporters:

| MAIL MESSAGE |

I'm sitting at a corner table in Starbucks in Lake Oswego, Oregon. It's raining outside. I wish you could sit in the chair across the table from me and enjoy a hot cup of coffee and an hour of conversation. But since you can't, I want to tell you how I'm doing.

Frankly, I'm not sure how I'm doing. I feel as though I've lived thirty years in six weeks. I feel the deep sorrow of grief and loss. Yet I have an indescribable sense of peace because I know God is in control. There have been days when I felt wrapped by the arms of God . . . days when I sensed His presence like no other time in my life.

On many occasions I've contemplated the words of God after He refused to take away Paul's thorn in the flesh. He said, "My grace is sufficient for you." I'd never known God's comforting grace because I'd never needed it. And now I can't possibly explain how astounded I am to bask in His grace—like a flower soaking in the warmth of the sun.

I'm also amazed that God has enabled me to forgive the man who murdered Bonnie. As the guards restrained me at the clinic, preventing me from seeing Bonnie, I suddenly knew what Jesus meant when He said from the cross, "Father, forgive them." In that moment I felt Jesus forgiving that man through me.

Another reality that moved from the abstract to the concrete occurred when I realized I had lost practically every earthly possession. Prior to Bonnie's death we both believed we had a fulfilling and fruitful ministry. And we did. We had many Lebanese friends who loved us; we had a beautiful apartment, a car, a strong support team, and the joy of touching lives for Christ. When I left Lebanon I had to leave everything behind.

Yet, and this still astounds me, I never crumbled. On the contrary, I felt a massive storm hit me full force, and like a castle built on a mountain of granite, I withstood the worst of it. Jesus proved to be all He said. I had built my life on the truth of His life, and He held me up when I could have washed away.

Thanks for your care . . .

The Bleeding Edge of Humanity

A year after Bonnie went to Jesus, I got this e-mail from my younger brother, Jonathan:

MAIL MESSAGE

From: Jonathan Witherall
To: Gary Witherall
Subject: Gary and Bonnie 21st November
Date: Fri., 21 Nov. 2003

Hey Boss, how are you?

I thought now would be the time to reflect and share my thoughts on Bonnie, you, and you and Bonnie. None of the following is just simply dressed up in emotion or in the hindsight of tragedy. I would have said any of what I am about to write this moment last year. HERE WE GO. . . . Operation Mobilization's tribute to Bonnie on the home page of their Web site started with the following comment:

Some people talk about being on the cutting edge; some actually live there. Fewer choose to dwell on the bleeding edge of humanity, where nothing is humanly certain except great need, where risk defies other definitions, where light shines the brighter for the enveloping darkness. Sidon in Lebanon is such a place, and Bonnie and Gary Witherall were some of those few.

I, too, always felt that way about you, that you are unique in that you do things others wouldn't dare or simply consider doing. When you left for the MV *Doulos*, the fact that you were off didn't sink in until I saw you off at the train station. I remember going home and crying! I missed you then; I still miss you now. I remember collecting you with Mum and Dad at Heathrow. It was great to have you back, but then it slowly became clear, you hadn't come back to stay. From then on, I knew there was something more important to you that I'd never thought I would see. It was a drive to follow God's call on your life. I remember you doing a rope trick and using it to represent the gospel—you had changed.

You said to me, "Jono, there are men, and there are people who try and be men." You were so right, and I still use this saying a lot. You also once said, "Some people talk about doing things; some people just DO." You are both of the above and have been a great example to me and others.

When I heard you had a girlfriend I wasn't surprised and was very happy for you. I remember we had the photo of you and Bonnie up in the front room at home. Next thing you got engaged, and there was a wedding planned for April. It amazed me that Bonnie seemed to have the determination, enthusiasm, and knowledge of God that you did. She had her own personality and opinions and never lived in your shadow. She was also wise and godly in character. This, too, inspired me.

When you left [for Lebanon] I knew it was going to be tough for you, as you told me it would be, learning to read, write, and speak Arabic.

For the whole duration of your stay in Lebanon, I had a picture of you and Bonnie on the wall above my desk at home. I used to pray frequently, "Bless them, Lord." Sometimes Bonnie and I would talk online. I was always concerned for your safety, and I used to brag to friends and work colleagues about my brother and his wife living in southern Lebanon. It always sparked conversation.

When September 11 happened I was VERY concerned for you. People would ask, "How are they?" I didn't know anything other than you were both keeping a low profile. I had this little mission in my head to try and have you both come back to the U.K. for a breather, so you could let your hair down for a couple of weeks. I was glad that I could help you financially at the time, making it possible for you to [visit].

[When Bonnie and I had dinner together after you left for Canada,] we had an excellent meal. We sat and talked and talked . . . and talked! I wanted to tell her how good she was [for you], not to butter her up, but to encourage and honor her. I told her about how we all really loved and accepted her so well in our family, and that she's so highly thought of, and a great blessing to you. I think the things I said to her were right and timely, and in hindsight I'm SO glad they were said.

When I took her to the airport, she said at least three times along the way, "I can't wait to get back to Lebanon and the clinic." Like you, Bonnie wasn't interested in being cozy; she wanted to get on with the job God called her to. [As I drove home] I began to understand what a real warrior of God Bonnie was. . . . This was a rare thing, and Bonnie was unique.

On November 21, 2002, I was at work, and Mum called, sounding sad and telling me to come home. Dad picked up the phone and told me something had happened in Lebanon relating to Bonnie. I went home and noticed [former pastor] Keith Crump was there. When I heard the news I was not completely shocked, as I had filled in all the possible gaps in my mind whilst driving home. That day's story, and the weeks beyond, were incredible. I will save those for another time. However, I would like to say the following in closing:

I was sad, VERY sad. [But] I knew that you were both doing what God had called you to do. Also the fact that God doesn't lose concentration for a moment, and in that time the devil could send someone to fire a gun while God's not watching. I concluded, and still know and believe, "God is all over this." I don't know exactly why it happened; I guess none of us do, but we will know in the fullness of time. For now I implicitly trust God. When a major shift takes place like that of last November 21, YOU KNOW God is moving big pieces!

You still remain as one of my heroes! You're an excellent example to me, let alone others, and a privilege to have as a brother. I still miss you greatly when you're not here (that's most of the time). I miss Bonnie too, and always will.

With love, and great faith in Christ,
Jono

The Journey through Grief

After my time in Washington, I flew to Germany and met with a friend and leader I had known since my days on the ships. Dr. Allan Adams is an incredible counselor, and we spent a week together so that he could help me process everything that had happened. Psychologists have come up with some insights that seem to be constant no matter what someone's particular "grief story" might be. I share these insights both to tell my own story and in the hope that others struggling with loss might be able to reflect on their own journey. I saved my notes from those sessions and find them helpful even now.

STAGES OF CRISIS

Precrisis: Life before my crisis was good. It was a tough situation to be in Lebanon, and Bonnie and I were aware of the danger and the high chance of needing to be immediately evacuated. We had discussed the realities of laying down our lives. It must be said, however, that we had no intention of this outcome and I would have left the mission field rather than endangering either of us.

Impact: The initial impact of Bonnie's death was huge in this case. At this stage in my life, I cannot even imagine another experience that would so devastate me. This was simply the roughest and harshest thing I had ever faced. But in all these things I had an unspeakable presence of God in my life—a clarity, focus, and ability to worship the Lord totally.

Disorganization: I went from having a settled life with an apartment, budget, car, and ministry to throwing a few things in bags and being pulled off the field. It was a terrible and traumatic experience. All around me people were going through their own grief and shock. I lost sleep and a regular exercise routine. I also lost a close team and beloved friends. However, I was held up by my friends and coworkers at OM, an amazing organization.

Trial and Error: I saw God do some great things in my life. I am still very fragile, but far stronger spiritually than I have ever been. I moved into uncharted territories as I began speaking. I wasn't sure how this would all play out in my life, yet I had confidence that God would take me through it step-by-step.

Resolution: When I was in the hospital after the motorbike accident they wanted me to use a wheelchair. I said, "No way!" and straight away began using crutches. I refused most of the rehab and was committed to getting better. Even though it was only six weeks since Bonnie had been killed, I knew I couldn't sit in a state of perpetual grief, nor would I allow people to tell me at what speed I would recover. I knew I needed to charge ahead as fast as I could, with the counsel of a few friends. It was quite simple for me. I either got up or cracked up. Since the latter was not an option on my agenda I decided to begin the process of resolving this grief straight away.

Reflections from 2003

According to the experts, every grieving person goes through these steps of adjustment—but how he or she perceives and lives through them varies widely, as you can imagine. Dr. Adams later advised: "The progress through the grief cycle is *not* one steady series of directional steps. They zigzag. You think you are progressing forward, and then you find yourself back. Then you move forward and then back again. The main point is a steady movement toward the new." Here's how it happened for me:

Shock: This was full-blown. I feel that I am perhaps only just now beginning to pull out of the shock of this experience. I lost immense amounts of sleep. I lost many of the routines that patterned my life. At first I found very little of value and have yet to find the laughter deep in my soul, which defines so much of my personality. But I know it will return.

Numbness: Again, this is something I felt on and off. It is still with me, even today. Perhaps it shows itself in the indifference I sometimes feel. I was offered the opportunity to preach and share and there was a sense of throwing off the normal intimidations. I simply stopped trying to impress people and I didn't really care if people were impressed with me. I did, however, take great encouragement from people who took the time to connect with me.

Denial: I saw the blood on the floor. I sat in a plane with my wife's body in the hold. It was reality I could not deny.

Emotional Outbursts: There were many times of agony where I could only cry. I found it hard to think of the grave, her photos, and letters.

Anger: I had a choice from day one: I could choose anger that would lead to hate, or I could choose forgiveness that would lead to my own personal peace with God. I chose the latter. I have no place for anger. If or when it might come up, I simply reject it. I choose forgiveness and *nothing* else. I still pray daily that God will help me in this so that I can live a life of radical faith even in the toughest moments.

Fear: I had fear that I was to be shot also, a fear of seeing my wife dead, a fear of things unknown. Allan asked me how I might want to deal with my fear. The only thing I could think of was to bungee jump. I knew that if fear ever came up, I would need to be aggressive with it. On January 1, 2003, my friend Mike—whom I had met while working at the bank with Bonnie—took me to a bridge in Washington, the highest bungee bridge in the United States. There I bungee jumped off the bridge into a deep gorge. As I left the bridge at sixty-five miles per hour, free-falling headfirst, I burst into tears. Somehow stepping out and following Christ had always been that way: risky. But I had always believed that He had me on a bungee cord. In a strange way, this really helped, although I have no plans to do it again. But I needed to do it because I refused to be controlled by fear.

Conclusion: I am now further on the curve, but look forward to pushing past into the term *normality.* I know in some ways this will come quickly, but I also know the sense of loss for me may take years to fully recover from. I am in no race. When I shared my thoughts with Dr. Adams, he gave me this helpful clarification: "An important point is the end of the process. I would challenge the idea of 'normalcy.'"

He explained that the end result is termed "loss adjustment"—the loss is always there. Nothing will bring Bonnie back. The hope I have comes from knowing that she is eternally secure in Jesus' arms. This allows me to accept the loss and embrace the new.

A YEAR OF HEALING

January 7, 2003

One week ago I jumped off a 250-foot bridge and dealt with fear with a bungee cord. Now, over these coming months, I need to live again . . . to find the laughter of the soul. There is no easy solution, and I have had too much advice from too many people.

Oh, God, please touch and protect my broken heart. I cannot bear the thought of more pain. May God have mercy on me and not allow me to be alone. I discovered that marriage, having a partner in life, takes the boring and brings laughter; it takes the day-to-day and gives warmth. To lose this is like getting into a frosty car for work at 5 a.m. when you should be in bed sleeping.

January 12, 2003

Budapest

I have been amazed by the response to my message [at a conference for missionaries]. I should say God's message through me. It has been a little exhausting. . . . Yesterday I spent an hour with Graham Kendrick. What a blessing. His music shaped my life in my teens, and here we are at eye level. He gave me some strong advice. . . . Lord, please guide me so carefully that Your name would be glorified fully through my life.

January 21, 2003

Two months ago today. These are the days of grief—the Emmaus road. Nothing comforts me. I see and feel Bonnie in everything. Everything has been stripped away. . . . Everything for Jesus.

Oh, Lord, I want to cry from deep within and challenge Your church. By faith today I cry out in agony for a thousand to replace Bonnie. Then, Lord, I want ten thousand to go. Oh, how I miss my wife.

Oh, that one of you would shut the temple doors, so that you would not light useless fires on my altar!—Malachi 1:10

January 28, 2003

I went up to Chicago with Michael Card on his tour bus. We had such a rich time of fellowship. I got to know his beautiful family, including his wife, Susan. As we parted he whispered in my ear, "I love you" as we hugged. It was as if Jesus Himself were speaking. [Michael] gave me a guitar. My e-mail inbox had grown to about 270. Today I trimmed it to 58. I am very happy.

February 10, 2003

In the air to Atlanta . . .

Man, I am so up. Saturday I went snowboarding on my new board. I spent the day in personal grief, and it hit me hard, but [it helped to be] riding the new snow.

March 10, 2003 (the first time I returned to Lebanon)

Aboard an Air France flight to Lebanon via Paris to face what feels all too foreboding . . .

Oh, Father, can You heal and lift my weary heart? I want to believe but am trapped in pain. I don't want to be single. I don't like sleeping alone. I feel the Lord's presence, yet my heart is so deeply heavy. Lord Jesus, come closer and reveal Yourself to me. May I be a godly man because of my faith in You, not because of laws I cannot follow.

March 13, 2003

In the evening Matt and I met up with my old team at T.G.I. Friday's. Emotions ran high—it was a beautiful time. Afterward we went to the rebuilt part of the city [Beirut] and drank coffee at Dunkin' Donuts. The reconstructed area is very European. . . . It's great to see people relaxed again.

March 21, 2003

Four months ago today Bonnie was shot dead while I was asleep. Over the past two nights bombs have fallen on Baghdad. The war has begun, and I am broken over all the grief, the pain, and the suffering.

I went to the apartment Bonnie and I shared. The joy and peace we had there was gone—only dust, only things remained. Her clothes in the wardrobe: only clothes. The bed: just a bed. I thought I might find rest there, as one who travels and returns home and rests in his bed. But no—I don't belong here. Perhaps this may help me to move forward.

We drove to the clinic and sat in silence in the room where Bonnie once lay. Allan Adams flew down to be with me. After perhaps an hour, Allan said to us, "Well done . . ." at which point I began to break down. Then I sang the song "Befriended" [playing] the guitar Michael Card gave me:

> *Befriended, befriended by the King above all Kings*
> *Surrendered, surrendered to a friend above all friends*
> *Invited, invited deep into this mystery*
> *Delighted, delighted by the wonders I have seen*
>
> *This will be my story*
> *This will be my song*
> *You'll always be my Savior*
> *Jesus, You will always have my heart*
>
> *Astounded, astounded that Your gospel beckoned me*
> *Surrounded, surrounded but I've never been so free*
> *Determined, determined now to live this life for You*
> *You're so worthy my greatest gift would be the least You're due*

March 22, 2003

We sat glued to CNN for much of the evening. Bombing Iraq is happening even as I write this. I do not know what to say—except may the false gods of war be smashed. . . . What is more disgusting than dead Marines displayed on international TV for all to see, including loved ones? Just as Bonnie's [death] was broadcast all over the Middle East and horrible photos printed in the papers . . . I found it difficult sitting watching buildings explode . . .

Here in Lebanon I received more than I came to gain. I also was able to give. Perhaps it is in the place of giving that I have been blessed.

April 19, 2003

Easter Sunday

"Amazing love, how can it be . . . "

I am reading Abraham Heschel, the Jewish philosopher. In I Asked for Wonder, *he says, "There are three ascending levels of how one mourns. With tears—that is the lowest. With silence—that is higher. And with a song—that is the highest."*

Today is Bonnie's and my wedding anniversary. Pain.

May 13, 2003, Imperial Beach, California

"After the fire came a gentle whisper" (1 Kings 19:12).

I am staying in a beach condo in Chula Vista. This is the fifth to last house from the [Mexican] border. Outside is the Pacific. It is beautiful to be alone, quiet. On Saturday night I stayed onboard MV Logos II. *Billy Graham just wrapped up a four-day crusade here—many responded. . . .*

These days I often wonder, Where am I in life? What am I really doing?

My friend Graham was robbed of $5,000 in the desert in Iraq. The team is pretty shaken up. A new believer Jamil was blown up trying to defuse a bomb outside a friend's house—two martyrs in six months. It's a tough time.

May 22, 2003

Yesterday was six months from losing Bonnie. Last night I clicked on one of the (it seems) 32,000 web sites about her. For a moment I saw an image of her shot. Thankfully it is already fading from my thoughts, but it terrorized my peaceful day.

June 23, 2003

Pain today. Time magazine has [come out with] an attack on missionaries in the Middle East. They make it sound like we were mechanically converting the poor Muslims. It is so ignorant! And there, Bonnie's picture. I am furious. I worked out, slept, and felt better; but it is like an emotional raping. . . . Sure, we wanted people to come to Jesus, but through a message of love, hope, and forgiveness—as well as the ministry of the clinic. No references to those things, though. I wonder when they will ever write about Muslims converting Christians and the mosques going up everywhere in the West.

"Jesus did not come to give truths, but Himself." —Michael Card, commentary on Book of John, "The parable of joy"

July 22, 2003

Teen Missions Boot Camp

Yesterday it was seven months since I lost my best friend.

I arrived here at 2 a.m. It is a sacred experience to think that this was an important time in Bonnie's life when she was sixteen. I spent a lot of time in contemplation. Yesterday I gave the evening message about knowing Christ in suffering, death, and resurrection. I played my guitar each time before speaking. This night I played the Matt Redman song "Befriended" and sang with tears over the last lines: "Determined, determined now to live this life for You . . . "

August 16, 2003

Devils Dyke, South Downs, West Sussex

Perhaps my favorite place in the world—broken clouds, breezy. This time last year I was here with Bonnie. What would she look like if she were here now? I miss her—but she is happy. So I must move on—slowly.

September 11, 2003

The world is a changed place. It seems everyone is reflecting today. "It" is in the back of our minds, watching the jets fly into the towers. The war in Iraq is struggling, but the images will be a reminder of why we're there. President Bush is fervent about winning a war on terrorism—but I secretly wonder if this is a battle that cannot be won. Bonnie and I watched on our TV. I cannot believe it was two years ago. Father, be close.

November 2003

I went to a church where the service was more like a funeral. How can they possibly expect to reach this generation?

I need a rest.

I need an apartment.

I need to get married.

I finished three grueling weeks on the road!

Someone asked me, "When are you going back to Lebanon?" I tried to explain that Lebanon is my heart, but that I would currently be a big target and do not think it is God's plan for me to go back and die. I don't think they understood.

November 16, 2003

I think all the time about the upcoming memorial service marking a year since Bonnie's death. I still think daily about how bullets pierced her beautiful face. I cannot run from it; but rather I must work through it. It keeps me very humble. Only the reality of Jesus matters.

November 21, 2003

So here it is. Last night I sat looking at the clock, reliving the trauma—I mean, how could I not? I am no longer overcome by grief, but I keep thinking about the violence.

Memorial service at Moody. Dr. Stowell preached on "The Cost of Commitment." The service was powerful and intense. I have seen this as a decisive day, a watershed. I WILL MOVE ON! Bonnie and the Lord would desire me to burn brightly. Lord, please do something extraordinary through my life. In suffering, reap a great harvest.

November 22, 2003

Shopping on Michigan Avenue in Chicago with Bonnie's parents. Al and Ann are still in deep grief. I cannot help them—it will have to be Jesus. In the evening we watched the Christmas lights go on. Then we had ribs. So good!

January 1, 2004

I'm at Michael and Susan Card's in Tennessee. Last night we sat around and shared photos and Christmas gifts. We watched New Year's in Times Square, but with some apprehension because of the Code Orange alert around the country. There were terrorist threats; I could imagine the unimaginable. I wonder how long the West will live in this luxury of freedom we still enjoy.

14

TO THE LIMITS!

As a deer pants for flowing streams,
so pants my soul for you, O God.
By day the LORD *commands his steadfast love,*
and at night his song is with me,
a prayer to the God of my life.

—Psalm 42:1, 8 (ESV)

Let me invite you to a place I love to go.

I love to find quiet places in the craziness of this planet. When I think of all the painful experiences that God has chosen to let me go through, I survive by finding a quiet place. I love to go the mountains; I am drawn to the beauty and cleanness of snow. I love to be high up and on a snowboard. It is gentle to the mind and soul. I long for it when I am not near it.

There is a silence and unparalleled beauty in the Syrian Desert. I love being at sea alone for days; I love the lost beaches of Sri Lanka. I remember the long walks I took on the coast of Kenya, the white sand burning my feet, and the cool waters of the turquoise-hued Indian Ocean. I love the South Downs in England, with their gracious, rolling green hills, oak forests, and country hedgerows that divide the fields, making them look more like a patchwork quilt sown by the hands of God.

I loved the hills of Lebanon, the mountains, valleys, and water-falls, part of a lost world few foreigners ever venture to explore. In fact, so few foreigners ever see more than what they experience from a tour bus, yet Lebanon is truly one of the most beautiful countries in the world. I loved to stand on the hills in southern Lebanon, looking into Galilee as a warm wind blew on my face, a haze fading Mount Hermon into the sunset.

In the hills of Lebanon, it's not unusual to see the Bedouin with their sheep or goats on the rocky slopes. They herd many goats that may be scattered over a half mile as they climb to the next pasture. They have highly trained dogs that respond directly to strange noises made by the shepherd.

I love to lose myself in the safety of a close friend, to share a good meal with good conversation. When I have these things, it is easy to live through the harshness.

I love the silence of a room where I can lay everything before the Lord and listen to Him. I love when I am struck by profound Scrip-ture that suddenly opens up a whole other arena of life. It takes time to get to this place, but for me it is a place I need to go. It is a place I have tasted and long to visit regularly. It is the longing of the lover to be in the arms of that one person. Nothing else is important, and everything seems to fade in comparison with His presence. I do not do it to obtain approval; I do it because I need to be lost in His arms.

Since the time I joined OM and traveled, I have seen many changes, maybe more than any generation before me. There has not been a name given to the current changes in society, maybe because so much is happening in such a short span of time. Perhaps it is simply easier to describe change in terms of the generation that experiences it: baby boomers, Generation X, Generation Y, and beyond.

Today we live in a world of Internet coffee shops, IPods, digital cameras, and wireless laptops. We live in a virtual world connected by e-mails, cell phones, and online chat rooms. In only a few decades the images of nations have changed.

No longer are drugs restricted to inner-city street gangs, but are now widely available in affluent suburbia. Once, pornography was found behind the counter or on the top shelf of the local bookstore. Now it is accessible for everyone, including children, over the Internet. E-mail boxes now fill with junk and spam and endless advertisements for Viagra. I receive several applications a week in the mail offering me credit cards so I can access the tens of thousands of dollars that I deserve. And what about television? It is now a stream of endless reality shows from finding pop singers to how to clean the clutter out of your house.

We live in a world of information overload. We no longer wait for the newspaper, or even the six o'clock news. Whatever we need to know is now available right when we want it on our computer screen. Reporters tend to filter their news through a worldview that often sees Christians as out-of-date and irrelevant. At the same time, the evangelical has moved from playing an important role in society to a place that's considered out of touch and fanatical. I have even heard conservative Christians compared to extreme Islamic terrorists. And missionaries? Clearly, the world believes that anyone who calls himself a missionary must be wacko.

Politicians cannot fix the struggles of man's heart, neither can TV evangelists. The answer is not found in religion, or on daytime talk shows, or in any of the modern technological advances.

I am convinced there is nothing here on earth—or throughout all history—that can help mankind more today than the message of forgiveness and hope we have in Christ Jesus.

He is the only answer. In the end, He is all there is. Bonnie died sharing—and living—that Message. To lose ourselves *in* and *for* Him; to love Him to the limits, whatever that means in each of our lives. This is His call to us.

Will we answer?

The Longing

What is my story that You want to use it, Lord?
Who am I that I can sit in Your presence?
Why do I find my heart driving to be in Your arms?
What do You want from me these days?
I want more, Lord.
I want to drink of Your wine;
I want You.
Please come close—
Let me feel You, let me sing to You.
Bring me to the quiet place,
Give me long years to praise You.
Help me be useful to You,
May my life in You impact Your Church.
It is You and for You I cry;
I want the real thing:
JESUS.

On December 31, 2004, I married Helena
Kachikis, a granddaughter of Roger
Youderian, one of the five missionary
martyrs in Ecuador in 1956. Helena
and I are eagerly awaiting what God
has in store for us on this new journey
together.

EPILOGUE

For just as the sufferings of Christ are ours in abundance,
so also our comfort is abundant through Christ.
—2 Corinthians 1:5 (NASB)

When I returned to the United States after Bonnie's death, I was bombarded with requests from television, radio, and newspapers to do interviews. I declined most of them. It wasn't my goal to entertain people for an hour.

I hated not being married and prayed all the time for a new person to share life with.

I could not have imagined the way that my life was going to turn out, but I see the Lord has still been faithful. After returning to the U.S. from Lebanon, I spoke at Moody Bible Institute in Chicago. There I met Helena one evening after a meeting. She told me that her mom was dying of cancer and that her grandfather, Roger Youderian, had been martyred in the 1950s in South America. She said that my testimony had been a great encouragement. I was immediately drawn to Helena and touched by her story.

In fact, Helena's mom had been suffering for two years. On December 20, 2002, her mom died, exactly one month after Bonnie was killed in Lebanon. Helena sent me an e-mail informing me of her mom's death. "My mom and Bonnie are having their best Christmas ever," she wrote.

We continued to encourage one another over the coming months, mostly via e-mail. Through the most difficult moments in my life, the Lord gave me Helena. She became an unexpected comfort and close friend—a real gift from God.

Believing the Lord was bringing us together, in March 2004 Helena moved to Atlanta where I was living. Shortly after she arrived, we participated in an OM mission trip to the Cayman Islands. On that trip, some of us—including Helena and myself—were able to visit Cuba. While we were in Havana, I asked her to marry me. On December 31, 2004, New Year's Eve, we were married in Atlanta. It was to be the beginning of a new adventure for both of us. On New Year's Day we flew to Europe for our honeymoon.

While in Europe, we took a train from Italy to Switzerland. We were sitting happily in our first-class carriage to Brigg, when a woman entered the cabin. I was slightly irritated. Why did she single out our compartment? There seemed to be plenty of space elsewhere. She was fidgety and her face was gaunt and weary. It was clear that she had a lot on her mind.

Looking out the window, Helena and I were awed by the mountains of Switzerland that had just come into view. The deep blue sky was the perfect backdrop for the enormous mountains that were covered in snow. We were caught between the awesome wonder of creation and the obvious anguish on the face of the woman sitting across from us.

I made a comment about the mountains, and our traveling companion said she was quite used to them. "I just came back from Vietnam." She asked us if we had seen any news about the tsunami. I nodded and looked silently out the window.

For some reason, she must have thought that we were safe and that she could share with us. Slowly, she began to pour out her story. She had traveled to Maldives on a documentary trip with her husband and two others on their team. Early the first morning they had woken up to a lot of noise. Before they could make sense of the sounds, the water had risen as high as their fourth floor hotel windows. One minute it was sunny, and the next, water was coming in everywhere. Jumping out of bed they found something to smash the windows, and the water flooded in. She would never see her husband or the others again. She was alone. Forced to stay there for four lonely days, she wandered through the devastation before being evacuated to Vietnam, where she was told to wait. Wait for what, a miracle?

She told us that she still couldn't believe it. She had not seen a body, and therefore experienced no closure.

I remembered the day that I had heard the news about the tsunami. Although I was thrilled about my plans with Helena, I had been forced to remember the reality of a lonely, broken place. Now here we were on our honeymoon, and this woman was on her way home—alone. I knew that the train was taking her to face her family and friends, and then, the long lonely nights. I knew from experience that her suffering was hard, but I wondered how much worse it looked to someone without any hope?

Helena shared our stories, about our own loss and suffering. And then she said that through sorrow Jesus had been her best friend. It was as if the Lord had set it all up for us to be in that same compartment, at that time. He wanted us to tell our stories and to share Jesus with a broken, hurting person.

The future for Helena and me is a blank page, but together we will burn brightly for the Lord.

MORE. . .

An Evening Looking Out at the Sun Setting over the Mediterranean

It was as if a master artist painted the skies
With all the colors of blue
Then like fine touches of a brush
Faint white clouds stretch across the lazy sky
As if reluctant to surrender

—Gary Witherall

The Last Person

Who is the last person you will ever look at?
Who was the last person Bonnie ever looked at?
It was not her parents who loved her
It was not her husband who could protect her
Or friends—she did not have any chance to say good-bye to anybody
It was the eyes of the gunman
And I wonder if she smiled at the gunman
I wonder if the gunman smiled back at her
A momentary exchange
And suddenly a straight face fell upon him
As he raised his gun quickly and shot her
What was her last thought?
Fear . . . terror . . . or was it that she could not say good-bye to
  anybody?
Was it His peace that the Lord would have given her?
To help her deal with such a traumatic experience
Did she have enough time to become terrified, or was it just
  immediate?
Did she think for such a time as this *Lord, I give you my life?*

And then of course, who was the first person to greet her
From terror to beauty
From horror to love
From self-sacrifice to a place of reward
A moment of complete aloneness
Similar to the aloneness of Christ on the cross
And Christ hung there
Whose were the last eyes He looked into?
Was it the eyes of the soldier that pierced Him?
Or His friends around or the thieves hanging beside Him?
Were His eyes on the Father—were Bonnie's eyes on the Lord?
Did she see Jesus standing there at the right hand of the Father?
                    —Gary Witherall

The South Downs: Devils Dyke

Written June 5, 1997, in Portland, Oregon

A soft breeze flurries through the long dry grass in wafting waves,
over the sides of the valley.

That is where my memory takes me.

Sussex in the summer with its old villages and lazy games of cricket
in the parks on Sunday afternoons.

The pebble beach at Brighton and the Pier where I would
walk and talk with Raoul.

Then there was the little pub at the bottom of Ditchling Beacon
near the fields where we used to camp for the downs.

Then the wonderful hills and roads around Balcombe

In particular the old narrow lane that wanders past the farms and
 fields where the family would go for walks.

But I guess my favorite place of refuge, whenever I return to Sussex
 in my mind, is on top the South Downs with a good friend beside
 me to talk with.

A soft breeze flurries over the long dry grass in wafting waves along
 the hillside.

That is where my memory often takes me.

–Gary Witherall

Only in This Life

Linda, Graham's wife, shared these entries from her journal with me a few months after we left Lebanon together:

> *November 28, 2002, 2 a.m.*—We should be boarding the plane any minute now to take Bonnie's body back to the States. Is this real?
>
> *7:45 a.m., Schiphol Airport, Amsterdam*—Graham and Gary beside me in the business class lounge, talking quietly about the consequences of what has happened. . . . Gary has been so amazing, so beautiful. . . . He cried as we went to bed. He took one more phone call and we lay and listened to soft sobbing. He is consistently bursting with energy and plans and possibilities. He has made it easy on the rest of us—he wants people around him and he talks and laughs always. Kamal said we're acting like Arabs, all being together and talking all the time and eating.
>
> It is exactly to the minute one week ago that I received a phone call from the pastor of the Mieh Mieh church: "There is a catastrophe at the clinic. Bonnie was shot dead in the clinic." I managed to say, "We're on our way" and with shaking hands called Graham.
>
> U.S. embassy, dialing parents to awaken them at 4 a.m., we make it through one night with hugs in the morning, Sami Dagher cleaned up her [Bonnie's] blood, Kamal reading to us about Stephen's martyrdom, Sidon memorial, ordering out, Mary Ligon bringing food and ironing, George Verwer, Franklin Graham, Dr. Joe Stowell.
>
> *12:20 p.m., high above Europe, heading for the United States*— Lessons of love being more powerful than hate and revenge. Did I believe that before? Especially with my cravings for "fairness" and "justice"? I wonder if I did.

Lessons of suddenness, Bonnie's slippers, damp towel, groceries from Spinneys, and then she moved through the veil into the unseen world. Am I ready? Bonnie was cold-metal violenced into the next world. . . .

[When we were alone with the Penners the morning of the funeral], Al said Bonnie used to hug him around the legs and say, "Daddy, I wuv you so much I can hardly bewieve it!" That's the bottom line—the suffering of grief. Yet Jesus says not to grieve like the rest of men who have no hope.

Bonnie's death continues to affect us, and I feel sobered forever. And sobering is good, the lessons learned are good. I look at Jesus in a more clear-eyed way. Graham and I remember, "Life is hard, but God is good." But I never stop sorrowing for Gary, that the loss lives with [him] in a way that it doesn't and can't live with us. After all is said and done, [he lives] without her. For that I am truly sorry. But John Piper writes, "But only in this life—only in this life. I want to be the kind of person who makes that 'only' what it really is—very short. Prelude to the infinity of joy, joy, joy—but not yet, not entirely."

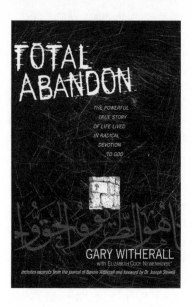

FREE Discussion Guide!
A discussion guide for
Total Abandon is available at

ChristianBookGuides.com

Visit Gary's Website at
www.TotalAbandon.com

To Schedule Gary for a
Speaking Engagement, Contact
Ambassador Speakers Bureau
(615) 370-4700
www.AmbassadorAgency.com

ACKNOWLEDGMENTS

I have so many people who have stood by me over these past few years. I would like to thank those who stood by Bonnie's family and my own family as they have been through so much.

I would like to thank the following people in particular:

Aden and Sally for their belief in me right from the start when I was still in my teens

My friends in Lebanon for standing by me in crisis

There are many who are life friends to me, of whom I consider Bill and Cindy Perkins and their boys Ryan, Dave, and Paul

I am grateful to the churches that have been behind my ministry: for Bill McLeod, Randy Richards, John Avant, Buddy Hoffman, and Mark Nonhoff

My appreciation to the Moody Bible Institute, Dr. Joe Stowell, Ed Cannon, and especially professor Ken Hanna who died of cancer in 1999—he had a great impact on my life while I was at Moody

Rick and Kathy Hicks and the OM USA staff who have adopted Helena and me as family here in Atlanta

Todd and Karen Hendricks for your friendship and support and for being world changers

My friends at Ambassador Speakers Bureau who helped me with meetings and travel arrangements over the past two years. A big thanks to Wes Yoder who went out of his way to help me

The great team at Tyndale House Publishers who helped this project be successful

Jan Long Harris who orchestrated the Tyndale team, Lisa Jackson for editing and encouragement, and Caleb Sjogren for your effort in making this a success

Betsey Cody Newenhuyse for all your hard work

Thank you to all who have supported me with finances and prayers and the many encouraging e-mails. You are a big part of my story.

Finally, thank you, Helena, for being such a great friend. You are the most important person in my life. I love you.

As a boy, Steve Saint lived among the people who speared his father to death. Rachel Saint, Steve's aunt, taught this jungle tribe to walk God's trail; in turn, they taught Steve to live as Waodani, one of the real people. Decades later, after building a life and career in America, Steve Saint is compelled by the Waodani to return with his family and live among them in the jungles of Ecuador.

The true story of an American family, a jungle tribe, and the healing and redemption they find at the . . .

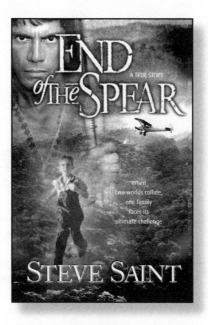

In January of 1956, five men entered the jungle in Ecuador to make contact with a savage tribe . . . and never returned.

Through Gates of Splendor, the best-selling missionary story of the twentieth century, was first written in 1956 by Jim Elliot's wife, Elisabeth. Decades later, this story of unconditional love and complete obedience to God still inspires new readers.

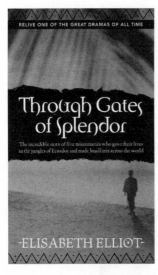

Mass Paperback
$6.99—ISBN 0-8423-7151-6

50th Anniversary Edition
$12.99—ISBN 0-8423-7152-4

Also from Tyndale House Publishers

An international best seller!
Experience the thrilling story of missionaries Gracia and Martin Burnham and their horrific year as hostages of the Abu Sayaaf terrorist group.

Hardcover $12.97—ISBN 0-8423-8138-4
Living Book $7.99—ISBN 0-8423-6239-8

Gracia Burnham reflects on her year of captivity in the Philippine jungle and the amazing lessons she learned about God's grace and constant care.

Hardcover $19.99—ISBN 1-4143-0123-5
Audio $22.99—ISBN 1-4143-0124-3